AIRBRUSHING
for Scale Modelers

AARON SKINNER

KALMBACH BOOKS

WAUKESHA, WI

Dedication

To my friends Jens and Robert, who showed me that modeling could be serious fun. Here's to the many days we spent building models, eating pizza, and watching science fiction. I still think we were onto something with our idea of a 24-hour hobby, fast-food, and video store. Thanks, guys!

Kalmbach Books
21027 Crossroads Circle
Waukesha, Wisconsin 53186
www.Kalmbach.com/Books

Published in 2015
22 21 20 19 18   3 4 5 6 7

Manufactured in China

ISBN: 978-0-89024-957-4
EISBN: 978-0-89024-958-1

Editor: Randy Rehberg
Book Design: Tom Ford

Unless noted, photographs were taken by the author.

Library of Congress Control Number: 2015930767

─────── P R O J E C T S ───────

Contents

Nothing improves the look of a scale model as much as well-airbrushed paint.

An airbrush provides smooth, even finishes with an ease that I could only dream about as I brush-painted a natural-metal finish on a 1/72 scale B-26, one of my early models. (That Marauder has been in a landfill for 30 years, and I'm willing to bet that the Humbrol No. 11 silver is still wet.) On the other hand, airbrushing can be frustrating, with failure leading to ruined models and the kind of language that might make a sailor blush.

My mother gave me my first airbrush when I was a university student and I've been learning how to use it ever since. Almost every day, I discover new ideas and techniques.

With this book, I hope to take the mystery out of using the tool and show you how to produce the kind of finishes and models you may have admired at contests or seen in magazines.

First, I'll describe the types of airbrushes, explain airbrushing basics, show how to use the tool, illustrate masking methods, and go over how to troubleshoot your work. Then, through 14 step-by-step, photo-driven projects, I'll expand on various airbrushing and masking techniques, which you can use on just about any model.

I'll also show you how to apply some of the more common paint schemes modelers reproduce on military aircraft and armor from World War II through today, including U.S. Navy three-color aircraft camouflage, German midwar armor, and U.S. Air Force 1960s camouflage. I even show how to airbrush gloss for a sports car from a favorite TV show and how to paint big-scale figures from a classic horror film.

Now, let's have some fun!

I n order to master airbrushing, it's important to understand the tool. Let's start by examining exactly what airbrushes are, how they work, what the different kinds are, and how to choose one.

Although airbrushes differ in design and construction, their operating principle is the same. Air under pressure creates a vacuum at the nozzle, which draws paint into the airflow and atomizes it. The scientific term for this is the *Venturi effect* (good information to know in case you ever find yourself on *Jeopardy*).

Single-action, external-mix airbrush

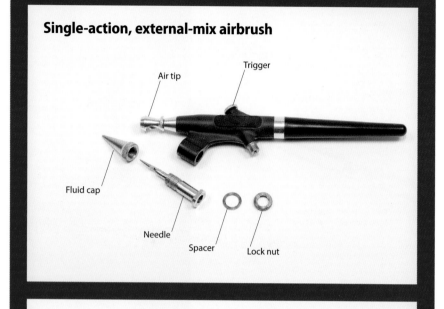

Air tip

Trigger

Fluid cap

Needle

Spacer

Lock nut

Single-action, internal-mix

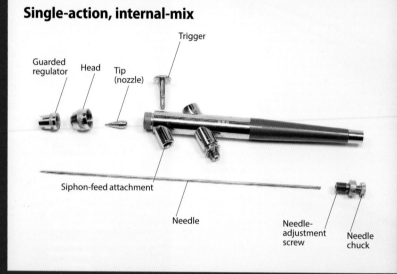

Guarded regulator

Head

Tip (nozzle)

Trigger

Siphon-feed attachment

Needle

Needle-adjustment screw

Needle chuck

Double-action, internal-mix

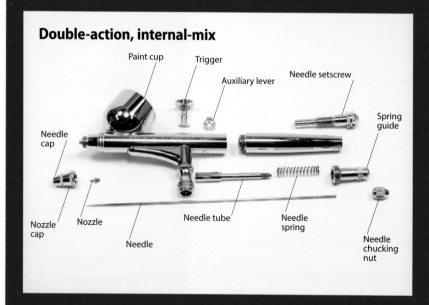

Paint cup

Trigger

Auxiliary lever

Needle setscrew

Needle cap

Spring guide

Nozzle cap

Nozzle

Needle

Needle tube

Needle spring

Needle chucking nut

The earliest devices, patented in the late 19th century, went by names like *paint atomizer* or *paint distributor* and were used by artists and illustrators. Nowadays, airbrushes apply fake tans, paint fingernails, decorate cakes, and put killer artwork on 1978 Dodge vans—and paint models.

While all airbrushes work by mixing air and paint, they are not all the same. They can be categorized into major subgroups based on how they regulate paint and air, where the paint and air mix, how the paint is stored, and a host of other features.

Single-action and double-action

Action refers to how the trigger works. Of all an airbrush's features, this one most clearly differentiates the airbrushing experience.

On **single-action** brushes, the trigger (or a button) opens and closes the air valve, **1**. This one action controls only the flow of air. The paint flow is preset by adjusting the needle's position relative to the nozzle before spraying, usually via a setscrew, **2**. A disadvantage of a single-action airbrush is that changes can't be made in the middle of a painting pass. Advantages are that you know exactly the size of the paint pattern and that there is a lot less chance of making a mistake.

On a **double-action** brush (sometimes called dual-action), pressing down on the trigger releases air and pulling it back moves the needle, **3**. Control of the paint flow is now at your fingertip, so you can make adjustments on the fly. But this extra variable takes practice to master and provides more opportunities for mistakes.

Many double-action brushes feature a setscrew, usually on the back end, that limits the needle's movement, **4**. This minimizes the chance of applying too much paint if your finger slips.

When describing the differences between single-action and double-action brushes, I often use the imperfect analogy of car transmissions. Using a single-action brush is a little like driving a car with an automatic gearbox, needing to worry about just the brake and accelerator—stop and go. A double-action brush is akin to a manual transmission, which introduces the clutch and gear stick to the mix. You have more parts to operate, but you have more control—and it's more fun.

Internal- vs. external-mix

Single-action airbrushes can be grouped by where the paint and air mix. Many single-action airbrushes, like their double-action counterparts, draw paint through the body of the brush. While called **internal mix**, the air and paint actually meet at the tip of the nozzle in these brushes. Another group, **external-mix** brushes, has separate paint and air nozzles, and they mix paint and air at the front of the brush, **5**.

I've found that internal-mix brushes tend to atomize paint better and have easier control of the paint pattern. On the other hand, there is no paint inside the body of external-mix brushes, so they can be easier to clean.

Gravity-, siphon-, and side-feed

The placement of the paint reservoir affects paint use, the minimum pressure needed for spraying, and sight lines.

On a **gravity-feed** airbrush, the cup is mounted on top of the brush. At the bottom of the cup, an opening usually feeds directly into the paint channel; if you look down into it, you'll see the needle, **6**. The primary advantage is that gravity helps move paint into the brush, so you don't need air pressure to do the work. A disadvantage is that the cup mounts on the brush's centerline and blocks the primary aiming view, which can be a problem when painting details.

On a **siphon-feed** airbrush, paint enters from below as it is sucked in by air flowing over the needle and nozzle, **7**. My experience shows that you need more pressure to move paint efficiently, which is not a major issue except when you need minimal pressure, such as spraying detail work or special effects. An advantage is having a clear view over the top of the brush.

Side-feed brushes offer a little bit of the best of both worlds. Depending on which paint reservoir is attached, either gravity or air pressure moves the paint. Most side-feed brushes come with optional paint cups and bottles, **8**.

While cleaning the airbrushes, you'll also notice a difference. Gravity-feed brushes have fewer parts, especially if the cup is integral with the brush, so there are fewer places where paint can be trapped. Siphon- and side-feed brushes have tubes and channels that connect the reservoir to

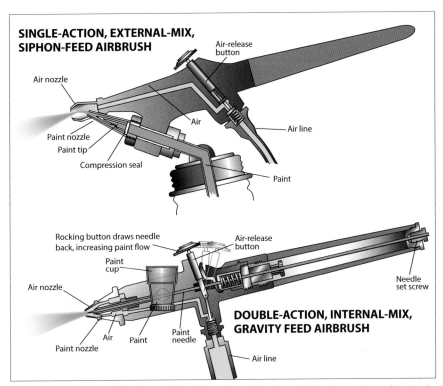

SINGLE-ACTION, EXTERNAL-MIX, SIPHON-FEED AIRBRUSH

Air-release button
Air nozzle
Air
Paint nozzle
Paint tip
Air line
Compression seal
Paint

Rocking button draws needle back, increasing paint flow
Air-release button
Paint cup
Needle set screw
Air nozzle
Air Paint Paint needle
Paint nozzle
Air line

DOUBLE-ACTION, INTERNAL-MIX, GRAVITY FEED AIRBRUSH

The basic anatomy of single- and double-action airbrushes. *Illustration courtesy of* FineScale Modeler *magazine*

the body, which means there is more stuff to clean, **9**.

Top button or pistol grip

Traditionally, operators hold an airbrush like a pencil and control the airflow and paint flow by pressing a button on top, **10**. The button presses directly down onto the air valve.

This grip gives airbrushing a similar feel to drawing or using a paintbrush, so it's instinctive. With practice, you can finely control the airflow by regulating how far the button is pressed. The grip can become a little awkward over time, and extended sessions at the booth can lead to hand cramps.

Pistol grips on airbrushes are relatively new. The air and paint are controlled by a trigger in front of an ergonomic handle usually built around the air valve under the brush, **11**. A single motion controls everything: the initial fraction of an inch starts the air, and then the needle starts to move and initiates the paint flow.

I'm a late adapter of the pistol-grip design, but now I find them quite intuitive and very comfortable to use over extended periods. But I don't like being unable to fine-tune the pressure with the trigger as I'm spraying.

Nozzle and needle size

Since the relationship of the needle and nozzle affects the volume of paint dispensed, the size of the nozzle is important. Selecting one depends on the types of work you intend to do. The good news is that many manufacturers allow for the needle and nozzle to be changed, **12**. Because they need to fit together just right for good paint flow and proper closure, it is important to use the correct needle and nozzle combination. Failure to do so can mess up your paint job or, worse, damage the delicate needle or nozzle.

Nozzles are usually measured in fractions of millimeters, and the larger the number, the wider the paint pattern. Some manufacturers, such as Badger, refer to nozzles as fine, medium, and heavy. Most manuals give some indication of the range of spray patterns—the minimum to maximum width of the pattern from a given needle and nozzle combination.

If you use only one airbrush, a medium (or .3mm) nozzle provides a good compromise with a range of paint patterns—from 1/32" to 1" or 2"—tight enough for detail work but wide enough to paint large areas. If the maximum pattern is too small, painting a large area can take an age and a day.

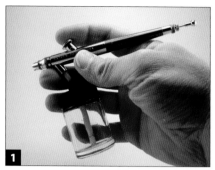

1

The Badger 200 is a classic example of a single-action airbrush.

2

The setscrew on the end of the Badger 200 moves the needle to adjust the paint pattern.

3

Typical of most double-action brushes, pressing the button on top of Grex's Genesis begins the flow of air, and pulling it back moves the needle.

4

The setscrew on the Iwata Neo TRN2 limits how far the needle can move.

5

The Paasche H is a typical external-mix airbrush. The paint pattern is adjusted by turning the fluid cap.

6

An example of a gravity-feed brush, the BearAir Peak C-5 has a integral paint cup molded on top.

Differing paint patterns is the primary reason many modelers have two or more brushes in their painting arsenal.

Air supply

Once you've settled on an airbrush to use, you'll need a way to power it, so you'll want a source of pressurized air.

Most beginner airbrush sets include a can of propellant, which is a fine source to start with. They're quick and easy to use, and quiet during operation. An attachment links the hose to the can with a screw-type fixture that opens the can's valve. However, you cannot regulate the pressure with any certainty.

I use a Testors can of propellant that is supposed to provide a constant 50 psi at 70 degrees Fahrenheit. But physics works against you: as the pressure is released, the temperature of the propellant drops dramatically (I've seen frost form on the can) and results in a loss of pressure. You can mitigate this pressure loss by immersing the can in warm water during painting, but it's an imperfect solution.

Canned propellant is a finite resource, so you'll need to purchase new cans peri-

odically. If you build a lot of models, that can get expensive. There's also a risk that a can will run dry during a painting session, which would be annoying to say the least.

Many modelers rely on small compressors, and most airbrush manufacturers sell them, **13**. They come in several styles, but single-cylinder diaphragm compressors are the most common type. They're noisier than propellant cans, but they provide constant pressure for as long as you need.

Cans of propellant and many small compressors don't include a regulator. To fully utilize all the features your airbrush has to offer, you'll need a regulator, which can be found on many mid-range compressors, **14**. Any moisture in the air will condense under pressure, so you'll also probably need to get a water trap to prevent water from spoiling your camouflaged masterpiece, **15**.

Some high-end airbrushing compressors feature a storage tank that helps smooth pressure fluctuations, **16**. The compressor only runs when the pressure in the tank falls past a set level. Modelers who do a lot of painting use industrial compressors, the kind found in auto repair

shops, that feature large storage tanks. While they can be expensive and heavy, they provide very consistent pressure, often at higher pressures unmatched by smaller units.

If compressor noise is a concern, consider using a tank of compressed carbon dioxide or nitrogen—think propellant can on steroids—available from party or chemical supply stores. The tanks themselves can be expensive and refills unwieldy, but they offer a silent air source capable of an extremely wide range of pressures.

Most airbrush-ready compressors come with hoses and adapters to suit most major brands. If you use an industrial compressor or gas tank, be prepared to purchase connections to adapt them to your airbrush.

Where to spray

Atomized paint weighs virtually nothing, a fact you can see whenever you airbrush. The air around the model fills with a cloud of paint that can float for a while. This stray paint can land in places where you don't want it to go, such as on an heirloom table. And worst, the paint cloud

7

The Badger 200 siphon-feed carries paint in a bottle mounted below the front of the brush.

8

Offering a choice of paint reservoirs, the Iwata NEO TRN2 comes with two cups (gravity) and a bottle (siphon).

9

The longer the distance between the paint reservoir and the nozzle, the more there is to clean.

10

Traditional airbrush design, in which the index finger operates the trigger, makes painting feel like writing or drawing.

11

Pistol-grip airbrushes like Iwata's Neo TRN2 are very comfortable for extended painting sessions.

12

Needle and nozzle sets increase the versatility of an airbrush by altering the diameter of the maximum and minimum spray patterns.

contains flammable chemicals that can be explosive in the proximity of flames or pilot lights. So choosing the right place to airbrush is as important as selecting the correct airbrush.

Proper ventilation is the number one concern, and if you don't want to paint outside, you'll need a spray booth. These boxes have a fan that pulls air from the booth, through a filter, and out of the building through a vent.

Booths are available in many sizes, and they differ in placement of the vents, **17**. The main consideration when selecting a booth is the volume of air moved by the blower, a measure of the quantity of paint being carried away. If the fan's motor doesn't pull enough paint, you can pull back from the booth and see a haze of color. (My old booth pulls so poorly that I've tripped the smoke alarm in my workshop, obviously not an ideal situation!) Pick one that sucks in a good way.

The size of the booth you need depends on the size of the models you build. If you focus on 1/24 scale cars, you should be able to get away with a smaller booth. If your preferences run to

1/32 scale B-17s, you'll want to spring for a larger one. The bigger the booth, the more powerful the blower motor needs to be to keep it clear of excess color.

Remember to change the filter regularly to keep the booth in tip-top working order.

Safety

I'd be remiss if I failed to mention precautions you should take to protect your health. Paints, even so-called safer acrylics, are chemicals, and most present serious risks from exposure.

A well-ventilated workspace and a good spray booth help, but you should also wear a respirator when painting. Dust masks are not sufficient; look for a proper respirator with interchangeable filters. The rubber portion of the respirator should form an airtight seal around your mouth and nose. Remember, if you can smell paint, you are inhaling vapors, **18**.

Latex, vinyl, or nitrile gloves prevent your skin from absorbing the chemicals in paint or thinner, and also help you avoid awkward questions about your RLM 70 schwarzgrun nail polish. (Yes, I know you'll

see photos in this book where I'm clearly not wearing gloves. I don't do it all the time, although I should.)

Finally, wearing goggles or safety glasses protects your eyes from splashes and inadvertent paint sprays.

Choosing an airbrush

A trip to a hobby or art supply store will reveal a vast array of airbrushes. So which one should you pick? That's the $1,000,000 question, isn't it?

You might assume that the versatility of a double-action airbrush makes it the best option. There's an argument to be made for jumping in with both feet, grabbing the bull by the horns, and learning the skills the hard way with a double-action brush. But there is definitely more room for error and frustration going that route.

Don't discount single-action brushes as viable options. At least three modelers I know produce beautiful work with Paasche H external-mix, single-action brushes. I routinely apply single-color schemes or basic camouflage with a Badger 200 single-action, internal-mix brush.

13 Testors Little Blue is a good example of an inexpensive, no-frills compressor that provides reliable power for airbrushing, but it doesn't come with a regulator.

14 Being able to see and alter air pressure with a regulator, such as one fitted to an Iwata SmartJet compressor, gives you control over one of the most important variables in airbrushing.

15 Water and paint don't mix, so fit the air line with a water trap to catch any moisture that condenses out as the air is pressurized.

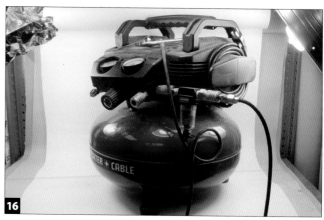

16 Designed for industrial use and adapted for airbrushing, this Porter Cable compressor has a 6-gallon tank and a built-in regulator.

17 Properly vented, a spray booth allows you to safely paint anytime without worrying about weather and wind. *Paul Boyer photo*

18 Safety first: gloves, goggles, and a respirator protect you from the toxic chemicals found in paints and thinners.

I also use Grex and Iwata double-action brushes, choosing between them based on the application.

Consider the kind of models you build when selecting an airbrush. For example, if you model World War II American armor—you can have any color you want as long as it's olive drab—then the uncomplicated operation and consistent results of a single-action brush may appeal to you. If you shun monochromatic camouflage in favor of mottled Luftwaffe fighters, the fingertip control over paint flow and airflow provided by a double-action brush is probably more your speed.

My advice is to talk to modelers about why they use the airbrushes they use. If possible, take different models for a spin. You need to feel comfortable with the brush you end up owning; there are few investments in the hobby that will cost as much and affect your modeling as profoundly.

U sing an airbrush means understanding and controlling several variables: air pressure, paint consistency, and distance from the surface. The key to achieving good scale finishes is learning how changing variables alters results and figuring out how to use those changes.

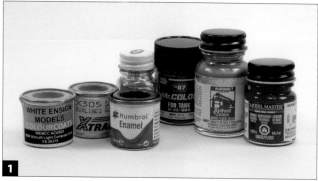

1 Some of the more established manufacturers of model paint make enamels, such as (from left) White Ensign, Xtracolor, Humbrol, Testors, Mr. Hobby Mr. Color, Floquil, and Testors Model Master.

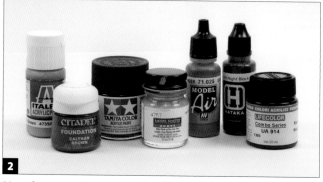

2 Manufacturers of acrylics, old and new, include (from left) Italeri, Citadel, Tamiya, Testors Model Master, Vallejo, Hataka, and LifeColor.

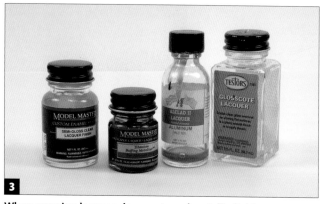

3 When spraying lacquer clear coats and metallic finishes, you can use paints by (from left) Model Master, Metalizer, Alclad II, and Testors.

4 Check the paint labels: they frequently recommend thinners and thinning ratios and even suggest spraying pressures.

Enamels, acrylics, and lacquers, oh my!

Paint is comprised of three things: pigment, binder, and solvent. Solvent keeps the binder fluid so the paint can be spread over the surface in a thin layer. As paint sets (dries) and the solvent evaporates, the binder undergoes a chemical alteration and forms a solid skin with the pigment suspended in it.

There are three basic types of paint for modeling—enamels, acrylics, and lacquers—with different binders and solvents.

Enamels, the old-school option, have been decorating scale models since plastic kits entered the market, **1**. Enamels contain oil binders and organic solvents such as petroleum distillates. Many of the best-known model paint brands are enamels, including Testors, Model Master, and Humbrol. I've found that different brands of enamels act much the same; if you've used one brand, you can use the same basic techniques for another.

Acrylics, once the new kids on the paint block, have caught on with modelers who favor their lower toxicity and cleanup with water, **2**. Acrylic pigments are carried by a resin binder. Although these paints are sometimes collectively referred to as *water-based*, that doesn't mean water is the solvent. Many use alcohol or glycol ethers as solvents. It's also worth noting that while considered safer than enamels, they shouldn't be considered nontoxic. When airbrushing, unlike enamels, different acrylics behave quite differently, and many come with a learning curve, so it's important to practice.

In the world of scale modeling, **lacquers** are commonly used for special finishes including metallics and clear coats, **3**. They contain harsh chemicals like alcohol, ketone, and toluol, and they can be aggressive to plastic and underlying paint. While enamels and acrylics dry on the outside surface first, lacquers dry from the inside out. This means lacquers dry very quickly. Differing formulations mean

lacquers aren't necessarily alike, and some are labeled as acrylic lacquers.

Pay attention to paint compatibility. You can't mix the three types, and it's also a bad idea to mix brands. You can apply one paint type over another with limitations. The rule of thumb is that acrylics can go over enamels and lacquers, enamels are okay over lacquers but can affect acrylics (test them first), and lacquers should not be applied over any other paint.

Paint consistency

Atomization is a function of paint viscosity (thickness) and air pressure. Although some model paints are pre-thinned for airbrushing, most are designed to be hand-brushed. They need to be thinned for airbrushing.

Thinner is any solvent that reduces paint viscosity, so what thinner you use is determined by the type of paint you are using.

I recommend using the thinner that is suggested by a paint's manufacturer, **4**.

5 Never use generic solvents—such as alcohol, commercial thinners, window cleaner, or water—without testing them with the paint.

6 Paint settles when stored, which leaves thick sediment at the bottom that needs to be mixed before airbrushing.

7 If you stir paint, rather than shake it, you avoid developing bubbles that can mar a finish. For the best results, keep mixing until the consistency and color is even.

8 Transferring paint with a rod, brush, or pipette keeps things neat and tidy.

9 If you pour paint from the bottle, wipe any off the bottle and the cap to ensure proper closure and prevent the lid from sticking.

10 I prefer to add thinner with an eyedropper or a pipette because, by using them, you can easily measure how much is being added.

11 Perfectly mixed paint and thinner produces an even, uniform film. Now, you are ready to paint.

12 If the film is almost transparent in the middle and thicker near the edges, the mix is too thin.

13 If the drop barely moves, the paint is too thick and needs to be thinned more before airbrushing.

You know it's compatible, and you'll be saved the disappointment and bad language that comes with ruined paint. In addition, many paint companies' proprietary thinners contain additives that improve paint flow. Once you are familiar with using a particular brand of paint, you can try other thinning substances, such as generic paint and lacquer thinners, mineral spirits, and isopropyl alcohol, **5**. But always test these thinned paints before spraying a model to avoid compatibility problems.

Thinning paint

Before mixing paint with thinner, it's important that the paint itself is properly mixed. Pigment settles as paint sits, **6**. Stir the paint in the bottle with a mixing stick until it has an even consistency and no thick globs come out on the end of the stick, **7**. Mix paint in a clean bottle or container. When mixing, you can also shake enamels but not acrylics—bubbles can form in acrylics and affect the finish.

Never thin paint in its original container unless you plan to use it within a few days,

as the thinner will break down and ruin the paint.

Transfer paint to the mixing container with a pipette, brush, or stirring rod, **8**. If you pour paint, be sure to wipe any paint from the threads to ensure that the bottle's lid closes properly and is easy to get it off later, **9**.

When adding thinner to the paint, don't pour it from the container since it's easy to add too much thinner or spill some. Instead, use a pipette or eyedropper, so you can control how much thinner you use, **10**.

For general coverage, such as the base coats on Tamiya's 1/35 scale Marder III, average thinning and pressure work well.

Painting details like the road wheels on Dragon's 1/35 scale T-34/85 requires close work, so I thinned the paint and sprayed at a lower pressure to avoid flooding the surface.

Common paint-thinner ratios

Paint	Thinner	Ratio (paint:thinner)
Floquil gloss enamels	Enamel thinner	3:2
Floquil flat enamels	Enamel thinner	3:1
GSI Creos (Gunze Sangyo) acrylics	Tamiya thinner, alcohol, distilled water	1:1 to 2:1
Mr. Color enamel	Mr. Color Thinner	1:1
Humbrol enamels	Humbrol thinner	1:1 to 2:1
Humbrol acrylics	Water	1:1 or 2:1
Italeri acrylics	Italeri thinner	2:1
LifeColor acrylics	LifeColor thinner	Pre-thinned, but add a few drops
Polly Scale acrylics	Distilled water	9:1
Tamiya acrylics	Tamiya acrylic thinner or alcohol	2:1
Testors Model Master gloss enamels	Enamel thinner	3:2
Testors Model Master flat enamels	Enamel thinner	3:1
Testors Model Master Acryl	Universal thinner	Pre-thinned, but add a few drops
Testors MM Custom Lacquer	Lacquer thinner (28016)	3:2
Testors gloss enamel (square bottle)	Enamel thinner	3:2
Testors flat enamel (square bottle)	Enamel thinner	3:1
Vallejo Model Color	Vallejo thinner	You will need to experiment
Vallejo Model Air	Vallejo thinner	Ready to use from the bottle
White Ensign Colourcoats	Mineral spirits/household paint thinner	2:1
Xtracolor enamels	Xtracolor thinner	1:1
Xtracrylix	Xtracrylix thinner	3:2

These ratios are based on my experience as well as the ratios posted by the manufacturers. These should be considered starting points for basic painting. Keep in mind that factors including the type of brush, air pressure, air temperature, and humidity can affect how paint sprays. Make adjustments as necessary.

So how much thinner should you add? Most model paint manufacturers print thinning ratios on their labels so start with those guidelines. For airbrushing, the right consistency of many model paints has been described as being the same as 2 percent milk. However, that's an inexact measure.

Here's a quick test that I find works 90 percent of the time when preparing paint for airbrushing. After mixing the thinner and paint, dip a clean stick, such as a toothpick, into the paint and pick up a drop of paint. Then place the toothpick against the side of the mixing container and let the drop run down into the paint. Properly thinned paint will run smoothly

and leave a uniform film of paint in its wake, **11**. If the paint runs quickly and leaves a faint trace, it is too thin, and you'll need to add more paint, **12**. If the drop hangs on the surface and looks more like a paint drip, the paint is too thick and needs more thinner, **13**.

Once you are comfortable with a formula for general painting—the one that provides good coverage and sprays cleanly—you can play around with the ratios to create different effects. When I'm spraying primer or one-color coats at 25–30 psi, I like using the 2 percent milk consistency, **14**. For detail work when I'm working close to the model, especially around tight spots, I prefer spraying at

a lower pressure, which produces less paint. Thinner paint atomizes better at lower pressures. It decreases the chance of excess paint building up on the surfaces and is great for subtle applications such as freehand camouflage and shading, **15**.

Before moving on to air pressure, I want to touch on thinning the newer European acrylics such as Vallejo. The Spanish manufacturer's paint is terrific, but thinning them for the first time, especially the Model Color line, can be frustrating. Model Color thinned to the consistency of 2 percent milk is too thin. You'll have to experiment to find the correct thinning ratio. However, if you use Vallejo's Model Air paints, they are ready to go straight from the bottle.

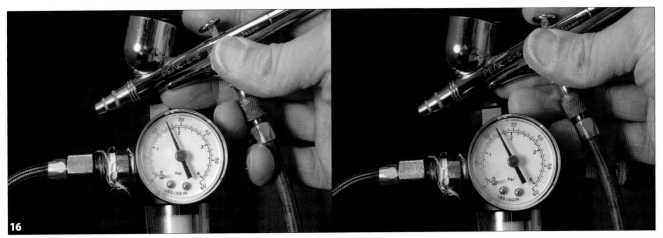

Pressure drops a few pounds per square inch when the button is pressed. To ensure consistent results, set your painting pressure using the lower number.

Spraying Tamiya acrylics at 40 psi through a single-action airbrush produces an even, dense line.

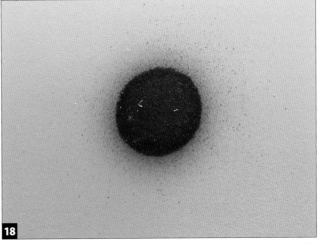

A dot sprayed at 40 psi is dense, but the edges show that it's right on the edge of being too much.

Air pressure

Of the many elements involved in airbrushing, air pressure may have the biggest effect. Deciphering those effects can help you work better, and to do that, you'll need to be able to alter the pressure. Regulators fitted between the compressor and the airbrush control the air pressure.

Regulators have a knob for adjusting the pressure, and most feature a gauge that shows the pressure, usually in pounds per square inch (psi). When setting the pressure, dial it to the setting you want and then depress the airbrush's trigger for several seconds while watching the gauge. With small compressors, especially those without storage tanks, you'll see the pressure drop as much as 5 psi, **16**. This number is the sustained pressure that you'll be able to spray at. I adjust the pressure with the airbrush running to ensure that I'm spraying at the setting I want.

How to use pressure

So what does air pressure do? Air atomizes paint and moves it over the model, so changing pressure affects the atomization and movement of the paint.

The higher the pressure, the more paint that comes through the nozzle when the trigger is released. The paint also atomizes better, which results in tighter paint patterns, **17**. But spraying more paint also means that it can be harder to control the amount of color that hits the surface, **18**. This problem is especially pronounced when spraying tight spots or delicate patterns, increasing the chance of mistakes and overspray, **19**.

Lower pressures mean less paint, so spraying is easier to control and problems like overspray and runs can be avoided, **20** and **21**. However at lower pressures, the atomization may not be as fine, so pattern edges can get ragged, **22**.

These variations mean that you'll likely use different pressures for different applications. Most modelers stick to 20–30 psi for general work, but some routinely spray at 50 psi or more. Then there are those for whom 20 psi is too high. I prefer spraying primer, base coats, and gloss finishes over large areas at 25–30 psi. For finer painting, such as working around details or masks, or producing special effects like post-shading or applying metallic finishes, I spray at 12–15 psi. At this pressure, I can control the paint better and gradually build effects without too great a fear of mistakes.

Not enough pressure

There is such a thing as airbrushing with not enough pressure. Enough air has to move past the nozzle to draw paint out of the brush and atomize it. I've been able to airbrush with the pressure as low as 8 psi

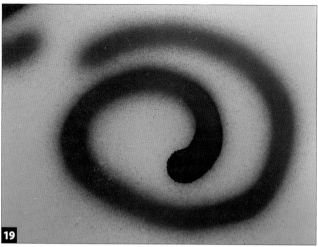

19 I started a spiral in the center at 40 psi, which looks good except for excess paint at the point of origin.

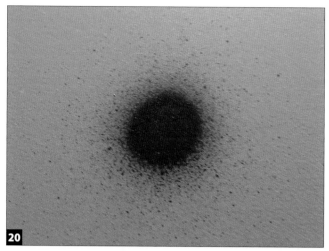

20 At 10 psi, the single-action airbrush produces an even spot without excess, but there's more splattering around the edges.

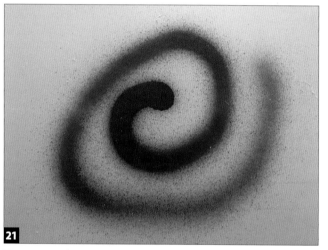

21 You can see the same splattering around the edges when spraying a spiral at 10 psi.

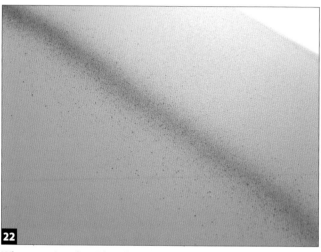

22 When moving the airbrush at the same speed as the pass at 40 psi, it's obvious that the 10 psi line is fainter and more ragged.

using a gravity-feed brush. On bottom-feed brushes, more work is required to move paint up the siphon tube, so they generally need a few more psi to work well.

With paint flow being a function of viscosity, properly thinned acrylics, enamels, and lacquers will airbrush the same. Experience will show you which paints airbrush smoothly.

Too little pressure can also cause paint to dry around the tip of the airbrush, leading to uneven spray patterns or a complete blockage. If you are spraying at a low pressure, keep a little thinner on a cotton swab nearby for cleaning the nozzle.

Distance to the surface

Much like air pressure, the distance at which you hold the airbrush from the surface when spraying affects the finish.

Paint emerges from the brush in a cone-shaped pattern. The farther paint travels, the wider and more dispersed the droplets become. Spraying at different distances can be useful in producing various effects. For general coverage, keeping the airbrush 3"–4" from the model's surface works pretty well. However, the pressure and paint consistency that you use can dictate the proximity of the nozzle to the surface. You may have to adjust your distance to be sure the paint reaches the surface wet.

Distance may be one of the harder variables to learn because many modelers err on the side of caution and spray too far from the surface. I suspect this may be because modelers are accustomed to using spray cans, which crank out a lot of paint and flood the surface. With airbrushes, you have better control of the variables, which allows you to get in close and ensure good

coverage without that risk. So don't be shy about getting in close.

Brush movement

A major caution with airbrushing is to always keep the brush moving. Spraying paint too long in an area floods the surface and causes runs. But what exactly does *keep the brush moving* mean?

It does not mean flying over the surface so fast that only a little paint hits any one area. Just as with gauging the distance to the model, you want the paint to get to the surface wet because the extra paint helps to level the color and provides a smooth, even finish. So slow down and watch how the paint falls on the surface.

Pressure governs the best speed. Using more pressure, and more paint, means the brush needs to move faster to avoid flooding the surface.

Mastering the tool

S o you've chosen an airbrush and an air supply, and we've gone over the underlying physics. Now, it's time to get down to the nitty-gritty of model painting.

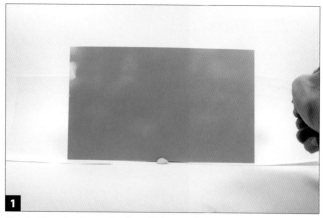

1

By starting the flow of paint off the model, you prevent accidental paint runs and are also alerted to any problems before committing paint to plastic.

2

Sometimes you can't start off the model, but it's a good idea to blow a little paint away from the model to prevent paint splattering off the nozzle.

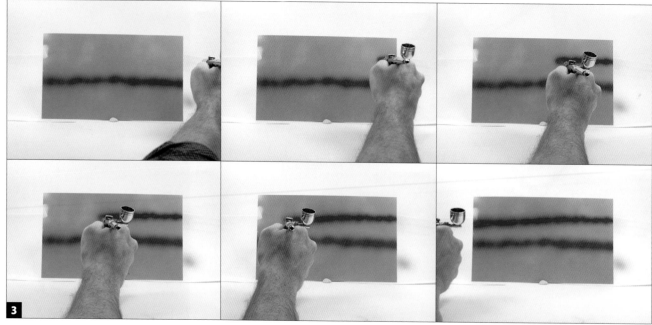

3

Start and end each pass off the model and keep the airbrush moving at a steady speed and an even distance.

Starting to paint

Always start airbrushing off the model, **1**. There are several reasons for this. First, if you start the flow of paint on the model, there is a good chance that you'll spray too much paint at the point of origin. By starting off the model, your brush is moving when the paint hits the surface. Second, and this is more often the case during a painting session than at the start, small droplets of paint build up at the nozzle and can get blown onto the model when the trigger is released, **2**. It is better to blow them out into open air away from the model.

Now, there are times when starting by painting off the model is impractical or impossible. I'm thinking of instances such as airbrushing camouflage or post-shading for weathering. You can minimize the chance of spraying too much paint by dialing down the pressure. To avoid splatters, trip the trigger a few times off the model to clear any excess paint from the nozzle. Then start painting.

Making a pass

To spray smooth, even paint, be mindful of two things: keep the brush moving, and hold it a uniform distance from the surface. When working at 25–30 psi, I hold the brush about 3" away.

Start the flow of paint off the model and then, slowly and steadily, move the brush across the surface, **3**. Paint flow, governed by pressure, dictates the speed.

You should move fast enough to prevent excess paint from building up but go slow enough to lay down an even layer of paint. You don't need to completely cover the surface on the first pass, but it needs to be more than a mist coat. Keep going all the way across the surface. Don't stop or reverse until you are off the model to avoid excess paint and runs.

If you are moving at the right speed, a good guideline is that flat paints should appear wet and glossy for a few seconds after the paint is applied.

Keep your distance

Maintaining the distance from the surface is easy when you are spraying a flat surface such as a styrene sheet. But, unless you are

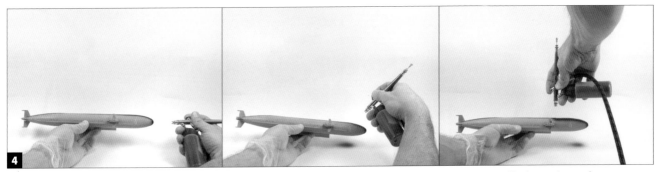

When airbrushing a curved object, change the brush's orientation so the spray pattern is always perpendicular to the surface.

Overlapping subsequent passes helps maintain a consistent density of color and allows the paint to dry at a consistent rate.

Starting with general coverage and then going back in to paint details often leads to applying excess paint. It is better to start with detail and recesses.

When airbrushing aircraft, the area between the fuselage and horizontal stabilizer on a Bf 109 is an example of the places I like to start at to assure coverage.

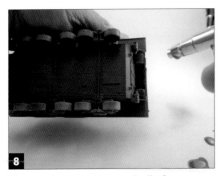

The overhang on the rear hull of a Sherman tank is hard to get at, so I made sure it was painted before airbrushing the rest of the vehicle.

I airbrush deck by deck while painting the superstructure of an Arleigh-Burke-class destroyer.

To paint a Mini Cooper, I airbrush body color under the fenders and along the engraved door edges first to be sure they receive a proper layer of color.

building a Borg cube, models aren't usually flat. You'll need to change the brush's orientation to keep the distance even and the brush perpendicular, **4**.

Overlapping the passes

As you finish a pass and start the next, overlap the last pass so the density of the coat is maintained, **5**. You shouldn't see thin paint at the periphery of the pattern between the passes. Applying wet paint adjacent to wet paint encourages leveling and avoids some of the problems associated with applying paint over partially dried paint.

Starting with details

Except for things like airliners and rockets, most models are a series of shapes with sharp edges, corners, and details. The challenge is making sure those features get painted properly without flooding the surrounding areas.

Generally, spraying the model before painting the details is a recipe for having excess paint and runs. So the key is to paint the details first.

After loading the reservoir with the model's main color, I dial the pressure to 12–15 psi and first spray the hard-to-reach areas, **6**.

These spots differ from subject to subject. On aircraft, I start with wing roots, joins for the horizontal stabilizers, and areas around engine nacelles and intakes, **7**.

For armor, spray around the running gear and suspension, under the fenders, around the tools and intakes, on corners between armor plates, and under overhangs, **8**.

On ships, these spots vary by type and scale, but generally, it's best to paint under overhanging decks and around fittings, **9**.

If you are painting cars, focus on wheel wells and fenders, doors and windows, and any trim, **10**.

11 Sometimes the handiest paint stand is … a hand. (I suggest your own.) It's easy to maneuver and control, but a wear a glove unless you want camouflaged fingers.

12 Paint stands hold a model steady and allow you to turn it for access and ease of painting.

13 Small cardboard boxes can be modified to fit particular models, and they are easy to replace after you cover them with paint.

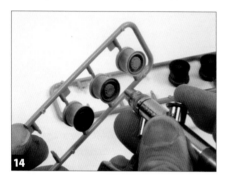

14 A convenient option, sprue makes a terrific handle for airbrushing parts. It's almost like they planned it that way.

15 In preparation for painting the floor of a Messerschmitt Bf 109, I attached several small parts including the control wheel.

16 I hate finishing a painting session and realizing that I've missed something, so I mark the sprue adjacent to the parts that will be painted the same color, as I did with this Bf 109 instrument panel.

Once you are satisfied that those spots are properly covered, you can turn up the pressure and spray the model for general coverage.

Holding items to paint

You should support models and parts during painting so you don't paint your fingers (or gloves if you follow my safety guidelines), mar the model with fingerprints, or bang it on a hard surface.

If a model is large or awkward, needs an overall coat of paint, or doesn't fit easily into a paint stand, I prefer to hold it with one hand during painting. This keeps the model at the right height, and I can easily maneuver it while painting, **11**. With an aircraft, I'll hold one wingtip and start painting the other. That way, especially if I'm using faster-drying acrylics, at the end of the painting session, I can paint the wing I was holding.

You can also use a paint stand while painting, **12**. Ideally, it should securely support the model with minimal contact while allowing easy access for painting.

Some handy stands are available from model companies such as Tamiya and Micro-Mark, but a cardboard box or bent wire hanger will do the job as well and can even be customized for a particular model, **13**.

For small parts, airbrushing them on the sprue is a terrific technique, **14**. The plastic frame acts as a handle, and you can suspend the painted parts across a box or hang them to dry. If I have small assemblies that need to be the same color, such as cockpit walls and engines, sometimes I build them on the sprue, **15**. Then I can paint them together using the sprue for support. So no parts get missed on the sprues, place marks adjacent to them with a marker, **16**.

The disadvantage to painting parts on the sprue is that they still need to be separated and the nubs cleaned up, which can damage the paint and require touchup. Also, paint affects solvent cement and super glues, so joining surfaces need to be scraped or sanded before assembly, **17**.

For parts with small holes, toothpicks make perfect holders. I prefer round toothpicks because they are stronger. Using them is as simple as pushing the tip into a hole until it fits snug and the part won't fall off, **18**.

Wooden skewers serve a similar purpose, and their extra length makes the part easier to handle. For parts with larger holes, try more than one toothpick, **19**. Or you can use a wooden stirrer with one end trimmed to a tapered point.

To support the parts during and after painting, use a piece of styrene or floral foam. The other ends of the toothpicks can be embedded in the foam for support, **20**.

There are several ways you can handle parts without holes. If it's a hollow or flat part, use a bit of poster putty or tape to secure it to a handle such as a toothpick, stirrer, or even a bit of stiff wire or brass rod, **21** and **22**. Or you can attach a lot of parts to a piece of cardboard with double-sided tape, **23**.

Brass rod or heavy wire can support an entire model if there is a place

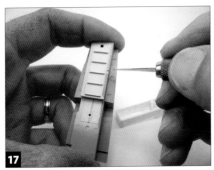

17 Glue and paint don't mix. A No. 11 blade is the perfect tool for scraping paint from the joining surfaces on an area of a wheel well from an F-4 Phantom.

18 A toothpick pushed into the prop shaft hole of this Messerschmitt spinner allows you to easily turn the part for all-around painting.

19 If the holes are too big for a single toothpick, as on these T-90 road wheels, try squeezing two toothpicks in; the wood provides enough give to allow a snug fit.

20 Save some foam packaging material to use as drying racks. Foam from around electronics components works well.

21 The wheels from Tamiya's 1/48 scale Buffalo lack small holes, so I used poster putty to support the toothpick handles.

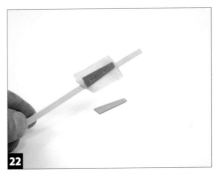

22 To paint flat parts, such as gear-bay doors, I tape them to a handle like this wooden coffee stir stick.

23 Double-tape pieces, such as this collection of T-90 details, to cardboard for painting. I keep a supply of scrap cardboard at my workbench.

24 Binder clips, available from office supply retailers and most desk drawers, are perfect for gripping sturdy parts like the gun on Pegasus Hobbies' aerial hunter-killer from *Terminator 2: Judgment Day*.

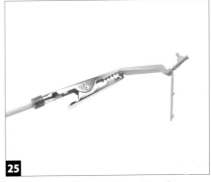

25 You can find alligator clips with other electrical supplies. The round wire holder is about the perfect size to hold a wooden skewer.

to insert it into the model. This handle works especially well with jet fighters; their exhausts present the perfect place to temporarily mount a handle. Wrapping foil around the rod improves the fit, if needed.

For prop planes, the hole for the shaft provides a spot for a wire or rod handle, but be careful when inserting a wire or rod to avoid pushing it through any interior structures.

Smaller parts and subassemblies with small tabs can be held in clips, clamps, or locking tweezers. I have a bunch of binder clips that work great for holding larger parts and even whole models, **24**. Alligator clips also work well to firmly hold parts, especially when you attach one to a skewer, which acts as a handle extension, **25**.

For a great, inexpensive part holder, flip the halves of wooden clothes pin; the

resulting clamp securely holds a part without crushing it, **26**.

For armor, openings for turrets and fighting compartments provide options for handholds, **27**. Some modelers mount a temporary handle by drilling a hole through the floor and placing a screw through it and attaching it to a wooden dowel, **28**. It's secure and allows the model to be turned in almost any direction for painting and weathering.

26 By flipping the parts of inexpensive wooden clothespins, you can make a clamp gentle enough for small parts.

27 The turret hole of this Sherman tank makes a convenient handhold for painting.

28 If you don't mind a small hole in your tank's floor, mount it on a dowel with a short screw for a sturdy handle.

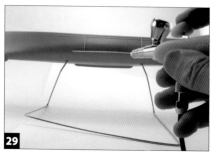

29 With holes for a display stand in the hull of Academy's 1/350 scale USS *Oliver Hazard Perry*, it is easy to install a temporary holder for painting.

30 You can bend and manipulate wire hangers to fit into almost any car body. And they're cheap too.

31 Scrub-a-dub-dub, plastic parts in a tub! I cleaned the parts trees from Tamiya's Buffalo before starting construction.

The holes in a ship's hull, used to hold its stand, can be used for mounting a handle, **29**.

Car bodies, usually painted separately from the interior and the chassis, should be supported from inside. An adjustable wire frame works well; ready-made handles are sold by several manufacturers, but a wire clothes hanger is a good option, **30**.

Surface prep

Even perfectly thinned paint sprayed at just the right pressure can't overcome a poorly prepared surface. Before painting, I lightly sand the surface with 1000- or 1500-grit paper. This smooths any minor blemishes in the plastic especially if you've used putty on the model.

The molding and construction processes leave oils and grease on the plastic that can affect paint adhesion. Acrylics are especially susceptible to these substances. Before starting construction, wash the sprues in a mild dish soap solution, **31**. Then rinse them with cool, clear water and set them aside to air dry.

Once the model is ready for painting, wipe it with rubbing alcohol (isopropyl) or something like Testors Plastic Prep to remove skin oils and other substances, **32**.

When doing so, don't saturate the surface, and be careful around delicate features.

Mold-release agents used to ease resin part removal are especially detrimental to paint adhesion, so it's imperative to clean them off. Submerge parts in Westley's Bleche-Wite, an automobile tire cleaner, overnight and then rinse them in clean water, **33**. After the parts dry, the paint should stick to them just fine.

Priming

Primer is more than just a base coat of color. Thicker and more opaque than standard paint, primer produces a tough base layer that promotes paint adhesion, covers underlying colors so the main colors look uniform, and can fill and correct small scratches or other blemishes. In fact, light gray primer reveals problems such as sink holes, unfilled gaps, and scratches that are often invisible on bare plastic.

Most model paint companies sell primer compatible with their color lines. Specialty primers, such as Mr. Surfacer from GSI Creos, are thick enough to double as a filler, but most only work on minor problems. Applying multiple layers of primer and sanding between coats smooths the surface and produces an even surface for color coats.

Whether to use primer or not is a matter of choice. I almost always apply it before spraying acrylics to ensure their adhesion. I use it less frequently with enamels, basing my decision on how much filler I used during construction. If the model features multicolored plastic or a hodgepodge of resin and metal, I'll airbrush primer to cover the mix of colors.

Some lacquers, especially metallic finishes, can be aggressive and craze plastic. Primer serves as a barrier against that problem.

Primer used to come in three colors—white, light gray, and red oxide—but now there are almost as many options as there are camouflage schemes. Primer color affects the overlying paint, so choose wisely.

Gray is a basic, neutral choice, but if a model will be yellow or red, white primer makes those colors pop. Dark primers—brown or even black—can give depth to camouflage and serve as a starting point for pre-shading.

Painting angles

Painting soft-edged camouflage and liveries, often applied to full-size vehicles with spray guns, is how an airbrush really earns

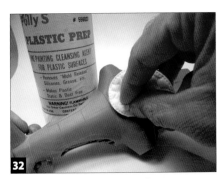

32

Using a cotton pad, I applied Testors Plastic Prep to Pegasus' hunter-killer to remove any impediments to painting.

33

I soaked the resin ejection seat from Eduard's 1/48 scale Lightning in tire cleaner overnight to remove any mold-release agents.

34

The basic pattern produced by an airbrush is thin on one side, much, much thicker in the middle, and thin again on the other side.

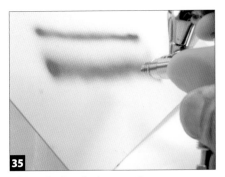

35

Tilting the brush changes the spray pattern, producing a less dense, feathered line compared to spraying straight down.

36

The camouflage on this LAV has color edges that are soft but not too soft. *U.S. Marine Corps photo by Cpl. Charles Santamaria.*

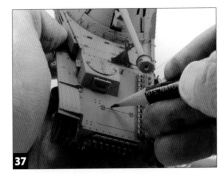

37

I roughly penciled the outline of the camouflage on Tamiya's Marder III. It doesn't need to be perfect, just enough to keep you heading in the right direction.

38

To apply mottled camouflage on a Messerschmitt Bf 109F, I gradually built up splotches from the inside out.

its stripes—and squiggles, splotches, and streaks. By using an airbrush's spray pattern, you can easily create this effect.

The spray pattern is denser in the middle and gets thinner and fuzzier toward the edges, **34**. When sprayed directly from above, the pattern is an even circle with a uniform gradient of paint around it. Tilting the brush from the perpendicular changes the pattern's tightness. The edge away from the brush becomes more feathered and loose, while the edge closest to the brush becomes much tighter, **35**. The closer the brush is to the surface, the tighter the near edge becomes.

When painting a camouflage pattern with reasonably sharp edges, start by painting the outline, keeping the brush pointed toward the center. The hardness of the demarcation should be driven by the full-size example. It should be soft but not fuzzy and in line with the scale you are working in. Think Goldilocks: the line needs to be not too hard nor too soft, but just right. NATO three-color camouflage on U.S. military vehicles follows a set pattern and is sprayed on by a person with a spray gun, which produces a feathered, not splattered, line, **36**.

Once you've completed the outline, you can fill the design from the inside. Penciling the pattern onto the model can work as a guide, **37**.

Another option for spraying irregular shapes is to work from the inside out. I start by setting the pressure at 15 psi and thinning the paint more than usual. Begin spraying in the middle of a patch of color and build the color out to the edges. I find I make fewer mistakes this way. This method works especially well for the mottled camouflage used on German aircraft, **38**.

Don't panic if you make a mistake or color outside the lines. Load the airbrush with the first color and touch up the edges. This method also refines the edges of color patterns.

Not all paints are created equally when it comes to the ability to spray freehand. Some have a tendency to splatter more than others, so it can be difficult to air-brush a sharp edge.

Color order

Dark colors are hard to cover with lighter ones. The best approach for painting multiple colors is to start with the lightest shade and then work through progressively darker shades. For example, if you are painting a Royal Air Force Spitfire in standard temperate day-fighter camouflage, spray the underside medium sea gray first, then mask and spray ocean gray on top, and finally spray on the dark green.

Certain light colors, notably yellow and international orange, are a bit translucent, and they should be applied over white for the best look.

It's impossible to discuss airbrushing models without mentioning masking. By its nature, an airbrush puts a lot of paint downrange and it's not always possible to predict where it will land. so, unless you are painting monochromatic blocks, you are going to have to protect an area while painting. It can be something as basic as an airplane canopy or a tank's periscope or as complicated as a three- or four-color camouflage. Let's take a look at some of the basic techniques and tools that will help you achieve the look you want on your models.

1

Tape is your friend until it starts pulling up the paint you worked so hard to lay down.

2

You can reduce tape's tack by applying it to your jeans and then peeling it off. Just be sure they aren't covered in cat hair!

3

Masking tape is easy to apply in straight lines. Just decide where it needs to go and press it into place.

4

A fingernail is a handy burnishing tool that is unlikely to tear the tape.

5

I always spray along tape edges before anything else. This ensures proper coverage and helps seal the mask against paint bleeding under the tape.

6

Peeling the tape against itself limits the strain on the paint and minimizes the risk of the paint pulling up.

7

The tighter you roll the tape, the harder the mask prop becomes.

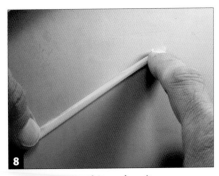

8

Position is everything when it comes to placing a roll of tape. It should be between ⅛" to ¼" behind the line being masked.

9

Don't press too hard on the tape because you need to maintain the tape's height above the surface to achieve an even pattern.

If you want a hard edge between colors, tape is almost always the best option, but choosing the right tape for the job is important. Traditional tan household masking tape is too sticky for the job, as it can pull up underlying paint during removal and leave adhesive residue behind, **1**.

Low-tack alternatives, such as blue painter's tape or Frog Tape, are less likely to damage paint. You can also reduce any tape's stickiness—and the risk of damage—by placing the tape on a clean surface and then pulling it off, **2**. A glass surface works well for this, and cloth is

a great choice if you want very low-tack tape.

These kinds of tape can be thick and may not conform very well to curves. That's when it is time to reach for specialized modeling masking tape, such as that made by Tamiya. Thin and transparent, it is flexible enough to go around corners and remains sticky on all types of surfaces.

If the line being masked isn't straight, the tape can be cut before being applied to the model as well as after. Always use a new blade to ensure that the tape's edge is as sharp as possible. If you trim the

mask on the model, employ the lightest touch necessary to avoid damaging the plastic or paint underneath.

To mask with tape, lay a piece across the surface, **3**, and then burnish the paint edge, **4**. You don't need to press the entire strip of tape tight against the surface. By only sealing the leading edge, you minimize the amount of paint pulled up when removing the tape.

After masking is completed, start painting by spraying lightly along the tape; the quick drying layer will seal the mask, **5**. Avoid spraying heavily at the edge of the tape or you risk bleeding,

10 The angle you spray at makes all the difference for raised masks. Most of the time, I spray from directly above.

11 A perpendicular angle produces a tight edge.

12 Spraying from behind the mask…

13 …produces a harder line.

14 It's unlikely that you'll ever spray toward the masked line…

15 …because it produces a very loose line and it's tough to control.

16 To easily paint a dot, cut a small, slightly irregular hole in a piece of thin cardboard. The hole should be a touch smaller than the pattern you want to paint.

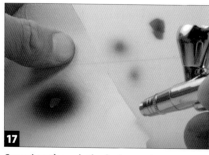

17 Spraying though the hole produces a somewhat soft-edged splotch of color. Moving the mask creates different shapes.

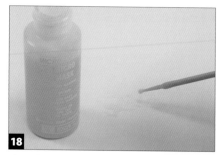

18 Liquid mask can be applied with either a brush or a toothpick.

which occurs when capillary action draws paint under the mask. Too much paint can also create a ridge along the edge of the mask as it dries.

When done, pull the tape back against itself at about 45 degrees from the edge, **6**. Remove the tape as soon as possible to reduce the buildup—I usually do it after cleaning the airbrush.

Other kinds of tape can also be used to make masks. I occasionally use Scotch tape and electrical tape, which is useful for stretching around curves.

Raised masks

You can also use tape to mask soft edges. The secret is keeping the tape above the surface so a little paint gets under it. Roll

a length of tape onto itself, **7**, and stick it to surface ¼" back from the edge to be painted, **8**. Add a strip of tape to the roll so that the edge is about where the color demarcation will be, **9**. The height of the mask can be adjusted by pressing the roll against the surface.

The angle you spray paint past the mask affects the line's hardness. Spraying directly down produces a neat edge, **10** and **11**. Spraying over the tape means less paint goes under the tape edge, so the paint line is a little sharper, **12** and **13**. Spraying toward the edge obviously forces more paint past the mask, and a looser line results, **14** and **15**.

Start any painting along a raised tape line with a couple of passes along

the mask. Then paint elsewhere on the model, away from the edge, for a few minutes, until the paint along the edge is touch-dry. Press the raised tape against the surface. It doesn't need to be a hard seal, just enough to prevent paint being blown past the mask as you finish the job.

A similar approach is useful for spraying dots and splotches. Cut an irregular hole in a thin piece of cardboard, **16**. Spraying through the hole with the cardboard slightly above the surface creates a soft-edged dot, **17**.

Alternatives to tape

Modelers have come up with a lot of unique masking materials, from salt to

19

Pulling up the liquid mask after painting easily produces chipped paint.

20

Talk about seasoned modeling! Sprinkle on some salt and manipulate it with a wet brush.

21

Like liquid mask, salt rubs off the model to reveal a realistically chipped finish.

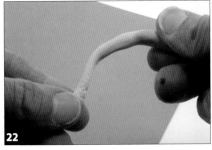

22

Sticky and removable, poster putty not only hangs stuff on the wall but it masks paint as well. It's easy to form to curves on the model.

23

Poster putty doesn't cover large areas well, so I back it with tape to ensure that the color stays where I want it.

24

The putty maintains its curve. As a mask, it produces a slightly soft edge.

25

Silly Putty is an incredibly versatile mask that is easily manipulated on the surface. If you aren't happy with the placement, just pull it up and start again.

26

The Silly Putty mask sits close to the surface and produces a tight demarcation.

27

I've been using the same blob of generic Silly Putty for seven years, kneading the soiled material back into the main clump to disperse the color.

Silly Putty. Whatever you use, be sure it can be removed after painting without damaging the paint.

Several companies sell liquid mask. Paint it over the area that needs to be masked and cut it with a sharp knife after it dries, **18**. After painting, the material usually rolls right off the surface. I have found success with it masking irregular shapes such as chipped paint, **19**. Rubber cement produces similar results.

Salt—yeah, ordinary, sprinkle-it-over-your-potatoes table salt—works much the same way for masking chipped paint. After painting the surface the color you

want to show under the chips, brush on a little water. Then sprinkle on a pinch of salt, **20**. You can easily push the crystals around the surface with a brush. Let the model air-dry and then airbrush the top color. Rub the salt off the model once the paint is dry to reveal realistic chipping, **21**.

I use poster putty (sold under brands like Blu Tack) and Silly Putty a lot. Both are great because they conform to almost any shape, plus they can be shaped on or off the surface. The difference between them is the hardness of the line created.

I roll poster putty into long worms and bend those to shape on the surface,

22. Backing the mask with tape protects against overspray, **23**. Airbrushing directly down on the mask produces a slightly soft edge, **24**. Most of the time, poster putty will not mark the paint, but test it with each brand you use to guard against problems.

Silly Putty works better on large sections, and it's easy to push and prod it into shape on the surface, **25**. Leave it a minute or two after application, and it settles into panel lines and other recesses. Be careful about adding more: this stuff sticks to itself a lot better than it does models. It produces a much harder edge than poster putty, **26**.

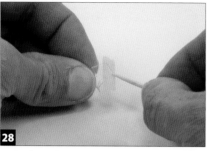

28

Round toothpicks are perfect for burnishing tape. The soft wood is unlikely to tear it, and the point pushes it into the corners with ease.

29

Always use a new, sharp No. 11 blade to trim away excess tape. A dull knife can tear the tape or leave the edge ragged.

30

The canopy frames on Italeri's 1/48 scale Dauntless are difficult to see, so I cut thin strips of tape to outline one pane edge at a time.

31

With the pane outlined, it's easy to fill the remainder with more tape or liquid mask.

32

Silly Putty doesn't mar clear parts, so it's perfect to support these delicate parts during masking.

33

Don't press too hard when cutting foil, just use enough pressure to sever the metal but not the backing paper.

34

It's easy to trace the outline of the frame with the tip of a No. 11 blade. Be sure it's sharp, or you risk tearing the foil.

35

Tamiya's 1/48 scale Brewster Buffalo includes a set of masks. I cut them out with a knife, using a metal ruler as a guide, and then lifted them off the backing paper.

36

The point of a No. 11 blade is prefect for precisely placing paper masks.

Both putties can be reused after masking. Just knead the used material back into the main blob, **27**.

Post-it notes are great for temporarily masking an area because they are extremely low tack.

Masking canopies

If you model aircraft, then masking canopies is a necessary evil. There are several methods you can use.

Let's begin with thin masking tape. If the molded framing is distinct, apply a piece of tape to the canopy slightly larger than the pane being masked, and burnish the frame line with a toothpick, **28**. Once the outline is obvious, trace around it with the tip of a new No. 11 blade, **29**. Then peel off the excess.

To mask indistinctly framed canopies, cut thin strips of tape and position them along the edges of the panes with the tip of a knife, **30**. Once the outline is complete, fill it with more tape or liquid mask, **31**.

Self-adhesive foil makes a terrific mask because it's thin, flexible, and easy to trim. To support the fragile clear part, press it onto a blob of Silly Putty, **32**. Cut a section of foil slightly large than

the area to be masked and peel it away from the backing paper with a knife, **33**. Position it on the part, burnish the edges of the frames, and then cut around them with a sharp blade, **34**. Peel off the excess foil to expose the frame for painting.

Another option is using the paper or vinyl masks that come with some kits or are available through the aftermarket. These can be printed, in which case you'll need to cut them out with a sharp knife, or precut to fit a specific kit. Peel them from the backing paper and position them on the part, **35** and **36**.

In this chapter, I'll offer some advice on how to keep your

airbrush running in tip-top condition as well as how to deal

with some common problems when they arise.

1 An ammonia-based window cleaner is good for flushing acrylics from airbrushes. However, don't let the cleaner sit in the brush as ammonia can damage brass, a common material used inside airbrushes.

2 It can get a little messy, but blocking the nozzle with a finger forces air back through the paint channels to clear them.

3 Sharp and delicate, an airbrush needle should be handled with great care. Place a needle in a safe place during cleaning, so it can't roll off the workbench.

4 By unscrewing the air cap, you can easily uncover the nozzle on an airbrush such as this Grex Genesis.

5 An absorbent paper towel draws the thinner and paint through the nozzle's tiny opening, which helps break up paint near the tip.

6 Always use the tools provided with your airbrush to remove the nozzle. Full-size pliers would crush this delicate part like a beer can.

Routine cleaning

Nothing ends a painting session sooner than an improperly cleaned airbrush, so every time you finish up at the spray booth, you should break down the brush and eliminate any trace of paint inside.

To properly clean your airbrushes, you'll need a few things: cotton swabs, pipe cleaners (the type sold for cleaning pipes, not for arts and crafts), interdental brushes, paper towels, and generic lacquer thinner. No matter which type of paint I use, I always clean my airbrushes with lacquer thinner, as it works on everything.

Before anything else, pour out any paint left in the reservoir and flush the brush with the solvent appropriate for the type of paint you're using, **1**. Spray it through the airbrush, cycling the needle in and out several times if you are using a double-action brush. Then place your finger over the end of the crown to seal it, being careful not to make contact with the needle. Press the trigger to force air through the paint channels and help clean them, **2**.

Next, slide the needle out, **3**. Be very careful when handling the needle and avoid hitting the tip. The tip will bend at the slightest touch, and it only has to be off a fraction to disrupt paint flow.

Remove the air cap to uncover the nozzle, **4**. If the nozzle is held in place by the cap, set it aside. If it screws into place, add a little lacquer thinner to the cup, then hold the nozzle gently against a paper towel, and let it pull out the thinner and dissolved paint, **5**. Don't press down, or you will bend the delicate nozzle.

Now you can remove the nozzle using the tool provided with the brush, **6**. If you use a tool not included with the brush, you risk damaging the delicate parts. Tighten the fittings with only finger pressure. Interdental brushes, designed to gently clean between teeth, are the perfect size for cleaning small nozzles, **7**.

Next, dampen a cotton swab with lacquer thinner and clean the reservoir and attachment points, **8**. Use the same swab to clean the air cap and crown, **9**. A pipe cleaner dampened with thinner reaches

the spots swabs can't, **10**. Never force a pipe cleaner through the brush. There is at least one rubber or vinyl ring inside the brush that you could push out of proper location.

Finally, squirt a little lacquer thinner onto a paper towel. Drag—don't push, always drag—the needle through it to remove any paint, **11**. Use the same towel to remove any paint from the body of the brush.

Now you can reassemble the brush. I usually spray a little thinner through it to make sure it's clean.

Color-change cleaning

You don't always need to strip down the brush, especially if you are spraying several colors in the same painting session. To clean between colors, first empty the paint cup and blow out any color left in the brush, **12**, and then wipe the cup clean with a paper towel or rag, **13**. Next, flush the brush with thinner until the spray is clear, **14**. It may take several attempts to get there, **15**. Finally, pull the

Interdental brushes are great for cleaning nozzles, as they reach all the way to the nozzle's tip. You can find the inexpensive brushes with toothbrushes and other oral care products.

Swabs can reach many tight spots, and it doesn't take much thinner on a cotton swab to clean paint from the bottom of the paint cup.

You can never have enough cotton swabs; they're useful for cleaning almost every part of an airbrush, including the air cap and the nozzle cap.

Pipe cleaners are narrow, so they can get into tight spots such as the paint channel. Be careful with them, though, as their metal core can scratch metal, so don't force them into the airbrush.

Gently wrap a paper towel around the needle, and then drag the needle though the paper towel to remove any paint.

Here, a paper towel catches the last drops of Tamiya red brown acrylic as I clear the airbrush for a color change.

Wiping the cup clean removes much of the paint, and it decreases the amount of thinner you'll need for cleaning the brush before the next color.

Generic lacquer thinner might react with the paint you just sprayed or with the next color, so for flushing the brush, I prefer to use the thinner recommended for the paint I just used.

Keep running small amounts of thinner through the brush until the stuff coming out is virtually clear. This indicates that very little color is left to interfere with the next shade.

needle and clean it with a paper towel, **16**. Now you're ready for the next color.

Full service

Before inserting a needle, it's a good idea to lubricate it. Iwata and other manufacturers make airbrush-safe lubricant. Simply put a dab near the needle's back end and pull the needle lightly through a clean paper towel,

17. The lubricant conditions the packing (O-rings) and prevents paint from building up on the needle. Only use approved lubricants. Products like WD-40 and machine oil can adversely affect paint or, worse, mess up the inner workings of an airbrush.

Periodically, you'll want to strip the brush further to keep it running smoothly. After removing the needle, air cap, and

nozzle, unscrew the spring guide freeing the spring and needle tube and clean them with lacquer thinner on cotton swabs, pipe cleaners, and paper towels.

Never soak parts in solvents such as lacquer thinner, which can break down vinyl and rubber seals, or window cleaner, which can damage the brass used in nozzles and other parts.

16 After a quick wipe-down of the needle, you are ready to spray the next color. I recommend working from the lightest to darkest shades to minimize the impact of any residual color.

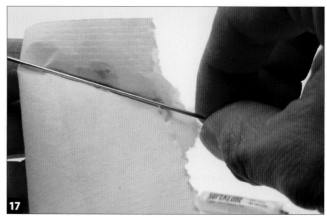

17 To help keep the brush operating smoothly, place a drop of lubricant on the back end of the needle and spread it along the needle with a paper towel.

18 A simple rack keeps an airbrush at the side of the spray booth ready for action. It also protects the brush from being knocked around and damaged.

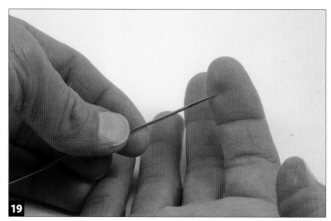

19 You don't need to press to find a bent needle. Any malformation will snag slightly as you pull it across your finger.

Airbrush storage

To keep an airbrush in working order, proper storage is as important as cleaning.

If you use a permanent spray booth, install a bracket or airbrush stand to hold your brushes. Make sure it doesn't put pressure on critical areas such as the needle, nozzle, trigger, or setscrew, **18**.

If your airbrush came with an air-cap cover, use it. These plastic or metal parts protect the delicate needle and nozzle when the brush is not in use or during travel. You can also reuse the packaging. Many brushes are sold in plastic, wood, or sturdy cardboard containers with foam cutouts that secure the airbrush and accessories. They make perfect storage containers.

Diagnosing airbrush problems

No matter how diligent you are about cleaning and maintaining your airbrush, and how gently you handle it, things will probably go wrong. Here's some common mechanical problems and how to deal with them.

Bent needle: No matter how careful you are, it is inevitable that the tip will get bent. I've dropped needles, caught them on models when working close, and snagged them during cleaning. It doesn't take much to damage one, and the smallest kink will disrupt the spray pattern. If you see spatters, check the needle for bends.

A bend may not be visible to the naked eye. If you suspect a bent needle, but you can't see it, drag the tip across your fingertip, **19**. Don't push the needle, as you could bend the tip more. (Worse, the sharp point may penetrate your skin, damaging the needle and leading to ridicule from family and friends.) As you drag the tip, twist the point against your skin. If the tip is bent, it'll catch on your skin.

Minor bends can be corrected by pulling the tip over a fine sanding stick or nail buffer, **20**. Angle the needle close to the surface and don't put pressure on it. Check your progress with a finger after each pass.

Major bends cannot be corrected—you'll need to replace the needle. They are relatively inexpensive, so you can keep a spare on hand. You'll be glad you did if you ding the needle during a painting session.

Split nozzle: Pushing the needle too far into the nozzle can crack or split the thin metal at the end of the nozzle. The result is uneven spraying and paint splattering. There is no cure for this problem, except for replacing the part.

Floppy trigger: If you haven't used your double-action airbrush for a while, the needle spring can bind. This leaves the trigger flopping back and forth instead of jumping back into position. To correct, undo the needle-spring housing and then screw it back into place to reset the spring, **21**.

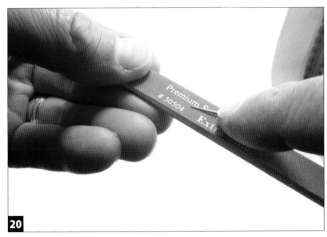

20

The tip of a needle is tapered, so be sure to keep it angled as you draw it across a sanding stick. Minor dings should disappear in a few strokes.

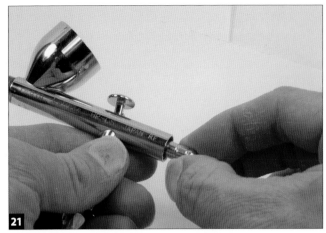

21

The spring returns the needle to the closed position when you release the trigger on a double-action airbrush. Loosening the needle-spring housing frees the spring when it becomes bound.

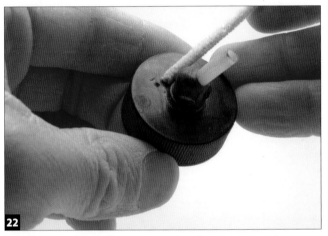

22

I used a little lacquer thinner on a pipe cleaner to open the vent hole in this paint lid after it became blocked with dried paint.

23

A little beeswax naturally seals the threads around the air cap without affecting the paint or damaging the airbrush.

Stuck trigger: If the trigger won't move, it's likely that the needle is stuck in the brush. The culprit is dry paint, so you'll need to clean the brush. If you can't easily remove the needle, add a few drops of solvent to the paint cup or paint channel, and let it soak for a few minutes to loosen the jam. Never force a stuck needle or use pliers or similar tools to remove it. This is one instance where the "use a bigger hammer" doctrine fails.

Trigger moves, but the needle doesn't: Tighten the needle chuck.

Paint sprays when the trigger is closed: The needle is not seating properly in the nozzle, so no seal is formed. Loosen the needle chuck and gently push the needle farther into the nozzle. Never, ever force the needle into the brush. (Did I mention the needle and nozzle are delicate?) If paint is still escaping, the paint channel is obstructed by dried paint or cleaning debris. Time to disassemble and clean the brush.

Air flows, but paint doesn't: This can be caused by one of two things. Check to see if the nozzle is blocked. If it is, clean the brush, and this should fix the problem. If not, the vent hole for the paint reservoir may be blocked, **22**. This small hole allows air to enter the bottle as paint is removed and equalizes the pressure. If the hole is blocked, the resulting suction prevents paint from being drawn into the brush.

Paint doesn't spray: The air cap is not sealing and allows air to escape. Make sure the cap is snug. (Don't use pliers for any airbrush connections; you risk stripping the attachments or altering the shape of delicate parts and ruining the brush.) If air is still escaping, apply a dab of beeswax to the threads, **23**.

Bubbles in the paint cup: The air cap is not sealed. Make sure the cap is snug or apply beeswax to the threads.

Dust and hair on a model

Unless you have a high-tech clean room, airborne particles will get caught in paint. To cut down on them, try to keep the area you paint in as dust-free as possible.

Here are a few other precautions you can take. Testors Plastic Prep eliminates static electricity, which draws dust to plastic. Going over a model with a tack cloth immediately before painting also helps. Misting water into the air around your painting spot can capture dust and lint.

When you see schmutz on your model, leave it until the paint cures. Then sand the spot to remove the blemish and smooth the surface. If it isn't too deep, you may be able to move forward. Otherwise, spray a little touch-up.

COMMON PAINTING PROBLEMS

As you spray your models, you may encounter paint-related problems. Here is how to solve some of the more common ones.

RUNS AND PUDDLES
Cause: The paint is too thick, or the brush is being held in one place too long.

Solution: First, check the paint consistency and add more thinner if necessary. Also, watch the speed at which you move the airbrush across the surface; never hold it in one place, and make sure you aren't too close to the surface. If a run or drip forms during painting, don't try to remove it by wiping off the excess paint or by spraying on more paint to try and level it. Instead, wait until the job is finished, sand the area smooth, and then repaint it if necessary.

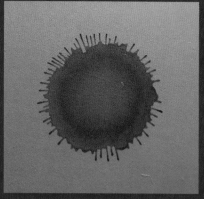

SPIDERS
Cause: With thin spots and tendrils of paint splayed out, spiders are a symptom of too much of something—or everything—including air pressure, thinner, or paint flow.

Solution: Check paint consistency and add more paint if it's too thin. If you need the paint to be thin, dial down the pressure and work quickly so the brush doesn't stay in one place too long.

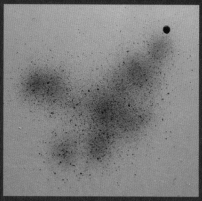

UNEVEN PATTERN
Cause: Damage or occlusion of the nozzle and needle.

Solution: Check the front end of the brush. There may be a buildup of paint around the nozzle or the needle cap. Run a cotton swab dampened with thinner over the area to remove the paint. If that doesn't fix the problem, it's likely the needle is bent or the nozzle is cracked.

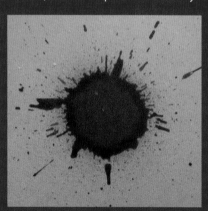

SPLATTERS
Cause: Collection of paint at the tip.

Solution: Clear the nozzle by spraying a couple of blasts away from the model before starting to paint. This is a common occurrence if you stop spraying for a minute, especially when working at a lower pressure.

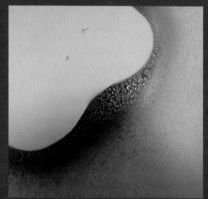

FISHEYES
Cause: Oils or other impurities prevent paint from sticking.

Solution: Thoroughly clean the model and loose parts before painting to remove any residue that may interfere with painting. Wiping the model with rubbing alcohol or Testors Plastic Prep takes care of most impurities. Fisheyes happen more often with acrylics.

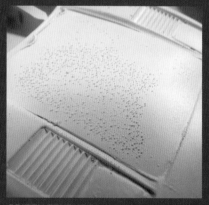

GRITTY TEXTURE
Cause: Paint particles dry before they reach the model's surface.

Solution: Get closer. This problem is almost always the result of spraying from too far away, which allows atomized paint to dry prematurely. Spraying at low pressure with minimal paint flow makes the problem worse. Move the brush closer and slow down a little.

Armor painting basics

I f you build World War II American armor, you can pretty much

paint it any color you want as long as it's olive drab. Modeling

Tasca's 1/35 scale M4A1 makes a great introduction to armor

painting techniques. This project provides a look at the sequence of

painting a tank as well as basic weathering. You can use the same

methods on any single-color tank including Soviet T-34s, early-war

German armor, and, of course, almost anything American.

1 Planning to use Tamiya acrylics, I first cleaned the surface using Testors Plastic Prep on a cotton pad to remove any skin oil left on the model during its construction.

2 I mixed 2 parts Tamiya olive drab (XF-62) with 1 part Tamiya thinner (X-20A), and then set the air pressure to 20 psi. Start spraying under the tank's hull, where you can check the pattern and consistency.

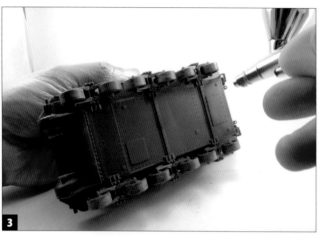

3 Spraying details like hatches and seams initially ensures that these areas are properly covered while minimizing the risk of spraying excess paint.

4 I painted the Sherman's complex suspension next. Painting the hull before attaching the running gear can simplify this process, but this involves more cleanup. I prefer this method for tanks with bogies.

5 To provide full coverage, keep moving the brush around the suspension arms, especially on the back sides of the units and wheels. Holding the model in your hand makes this kind of maneuver easy.

6 On the hull, I airbrushed around details like the appliqué armor plates, skirt attachment rail, tools, filler caps, and engine plates.

7 While airbrushing details, keep the brush moving and watch for excess paint. When working this close, it's easy to apply too much paint, so consider dialing the pressure down a little to spray less paint.

8 After the details were painted, I backed away from the surface an inch or two to widen the pattern, and then turned the pressure to 25 psi to paint the entire model.

9 After the details are painted, you can paint the model in smooth, even, overlapping strokes for widespread coverage. The focus here is on producing a uniform finish.

10 For best coverage, keep turning the model and make sure the brush is perpendicular to the surface at all times.

11 Use the same process to paint the turret, starting with details like the periscope, mantlet, vents, and hatches. I dialed the pressure back to 20 psi for this work.

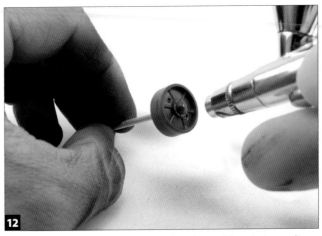

12 I mounted the road wheels on toothpicks to airbrush them olive drab, with the pressure set at 15 psi.

13 Without using primer, body paint can reveal surface problems. You can see where I blemished the hull with glue when I misaligned an armor plate during construction.

14 After sanding the marred area smooth, I airbrushed Tamiya olive drab to cover the spot.

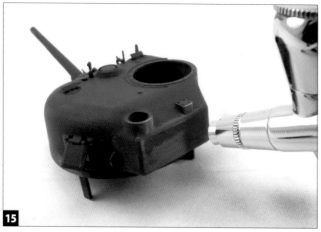

15 The seam on the turret bustle also needed some touch-up, so I carefully sprayed fine overlapping lines across the surface.

16 Even the smoothest airbrushed finish is a little rough, usually because the paint partially dries before reaching the surface. It is best to remove it now, or it will affect subsequent layers and exacerbate the effect.

17 Most of the time, you can remove it by lightly sanding the surface with 2000-grit sandpaper. Maintain light pressure so you don't go through the paint.

18 Sanding every surface will ensure better paint, and it doesn't take much work. There are no shortcuts when painting models, so it's best to take the time and get it right.

19 I removed sanding debris from the surface with a tack cloth. You don't need to press or rub. Just lightly drag the cloth over the model, taking care not to snag delicate parts.

20 Decals stick better to gloss surfaces. I sprayed the Sherman with equal parts of Tamiya clear gloss and Tamiya thinner at 20 psi. Building this thin paint up in light layers keeps the finish smooth.

21 Working slowly helps prevent drips or runs. After several light passes, the turret, wheels, and hull appear shiny.

22 No matter how good you are, some things can't be airbrushed. I placed a little NTO black (XF-69) and thinner on a plastic lid to hand-paint the road-wheel tires. To keep the finish smooth, wet the bristles with thinner before dipping the brush in the paint.

23 On a model, hand-painting parts like the tools is a matter of having a steady hand. Don't be too worried about getting the color all the way under the parts, as the dark body color will hide any shortfall as a shadow.

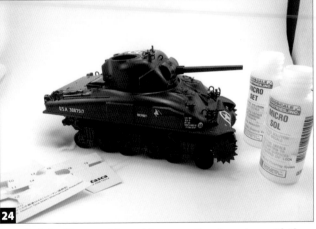

24 I applied the Sherman kit markings over the clear gloss with the help of Microscale Micro Set and Micro Sol decal solutions.

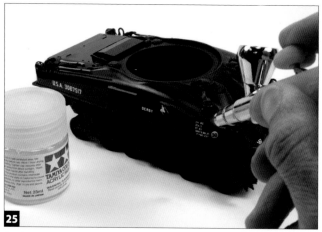

25 Sealing the decals with another layer of Tamiya clear gloss prevents damage from weathering layers and smooths the edges.

26 The clear gloss allows artist's oil washes to flow along panel lines and around details. I mixed a dab of burnt umber with Turpenoid for the wash.

27 Once the wash dries—I usually give it a few days—I sprayed the model with Tamiya clear flat (XF-86).

28 The model looks so nice and neat now, but tanks are rarely showroom fresh. It's time to add dust and dirt, something an airbrush excels at.

29 First comes a level of dust kicked up by the running gear. I mixed a couple of drops of Tamiya flat earth (XF-52) into clear flat…

30 …and carefully stirred it. The mix should look like tinted clear. The denser the color, the heavier the effect is.

31 I thin dust paints more than the overall coats—using 50–60 percent thinner—so the paint goes on light and flows around details.

32 Mist this mixture over the lower reaches of the tank, starting around the suspension. The great thing about using this thin, faintly tinted paint is that you can build the effect gradually.

33 I sprayed the dust layer around the Sherman's transmission cover, especially around the recesses and corners. When adding grime, think about the spots where dirt collects and use photos for reference.

34 Tank tracks churn up a lot of dust, and much of it settles around the rear panels. I sprayed a heavy dust layer around the idler attachment points and the engine access doors.

35 To finish, I sprayed light, quick passes along the sides of the hull to add a light film with a feathered upper edge.

36 To add interest and variation, I mixed another dust coat with Tamiya wooden deck tan (XF-78), clear flat, and thinner. I sprayed splotches around the suspension and added vertical streaks on the hull sides.

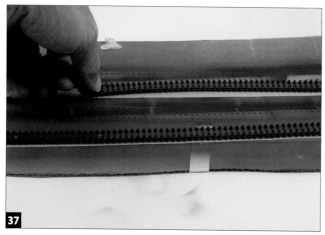

37

Tasca's Sherman comes with vinyl track. To paint it, I attached the runs to a piece of cardboard with loops of tape.

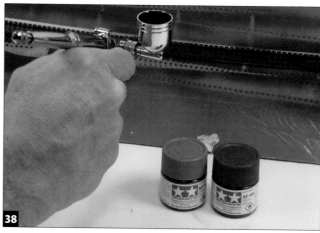

38

On a prototype Sherman, these tracks were rubber blocks with metal end connectors. To achieve a weathered rubber look, I airbrushed them with NATO black mixed with a few drops of flat earth.

39

After 10 minutes, I flipped the tracks over and pressed them lightly onto the tape…

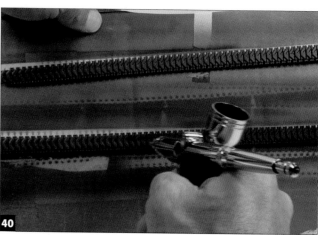

40

…and sprayed the outer surfaces with the same weathered rubber mixture. Keeping the pressure at 15 psi avoids blowing the track off the tape.

41

It was easy to hand-paint the metal end connectors with a mix of brown and gun metal.

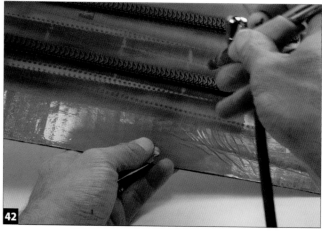

42

A misted coat of wooden deck tan and clear flat weathered the tracks and tied them into the tank.

Airbrushing single-color aircraft

B etween the bright yellow-wing finishes of the 1930s and the
blues of World War II, U.S. Navy aircraft wore an overall light
gull gray camouflage. Tamiya's 1/48 scale Brewster Buffalo
includes markings for that scheme, so it makes a perfect introduction
to basic aircraft painting. I painted and built the interior and engine,
and masked the canopy with the set provided in the kit.

1

The Buffalo's close-fitting cowl necessitated painting before closing the fuselage. But that big opening exposes the finished power plant, so it needed to be masked.

2

Taping off the hole can be difficult and time consuming. Instead, I traced the shape of the cowl—the exterior, not the interior—onto thin cardboard. An index card or file folder is the perfect weight for this.

3

After cutting out the circle—there's no need to be a perfectionist—I cut halfway through the circle.

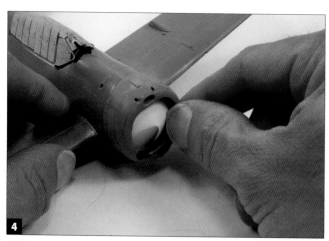

4

I folded the circle into a cone so it fit into the cowl opening and inserted it. When you release it, the cone opens to fill the opening tight enough to mask the engine.

5

I painted the Buffalo's wheel wells, so they also needed to be masked. After laying Tamiya tape into the long openings in the wings, I pushed the tape in place with a toothpick.

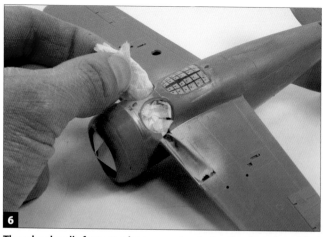

6

The wheel wells feature a large opening in the fuselage. I wadded bits of paper towel and pressed them into the wells. The soft paper fit tightly without damaging the model.

7 The first step in painting the exterior actually involves the interior. I airbrushed the cockpit color, Model Master aluminum, over the canopy and belly window, so the inside of the frame matches the interior.

8 The aluminum paint revealed a few fit problems around the canopy. I built up the dorsal fuselage with putty and sanded it to match the canopy. I filled other gaps with super glue.

9 I sprayed on another layer of aluminum to check the repairs and to ensure that the interior of the canopy looked uniform.

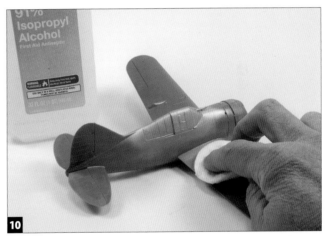

10 Skin oils have less impact on enamels, but it's still a good idea to clean the surface before painting. I applied isopropyl alcohol with a cotton wipe and left the model to air-dry.

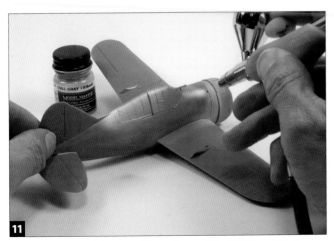

11 After mixing Model Master flat gull gray (No. 1930) and Testors enamel thinner, I airbrushed tight corners such as the wing roots and cowl edge. I used a double-action, gravity-feed airbrush, with the pressure set to 15 psi.

12 Keep working on the details and other spots, such as the machine-gun bulges on top of the wings, to provide even coverage. I kept the pattern narrow for this. You can use the setscrew to limit needle travel.

13 While the pressure was low, I sprayed the cowl opening. Changing the angle ensures that the inside edge of the lip gets painted.

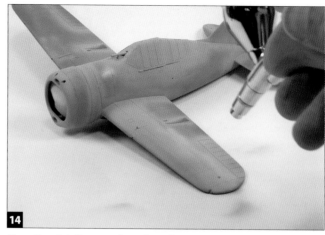

14 Once the details were done, I set the pressure to 25 psi and sprayed the Buffalo's surfaces with a wider pattern. Keep the brush about 2" above the surface and steadily moving.

15 Each pass should slightly overlap the previous one. Laying fresh paint over a still-wet layer helps them blend and level.

16 Leading edges can be missed when painting the main surface areas. Always take more time to airbrush the edges.

17 Once I think the entire model is done, I always go over it one more time to make sure that it is completely and evenly covered. Here, I am using a binder clip as a handle.

18 A problem with one-color schemes is finding a place for the model to dry without a freshly painted spot touching something. I stuck a toothpick in the tail wheel hole to prop up the Buffalo for drying.

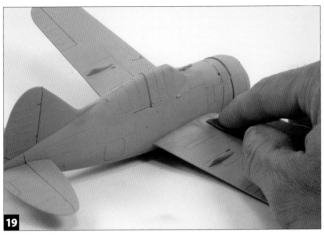

19

Before moving forward, I sanded the model with Tamiya 2000-grit paper. Wing roots can be very gritty because of swirling air and paint that deposits dry paint particles on the surface.

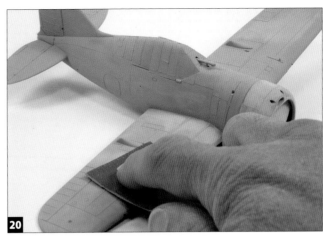

20

Even large surfaces can get a little rough. A quick pass with the 2000-grit sandpaper is all that's needed to smooth the paint.

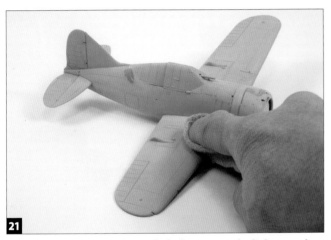

21

Rubbing the surface with a tack cloth removes the light, powdery sanding debris. You can see spots behind the cockpit and on the cowl where I sanded through the paint to correct problems revealed by the gray paint.

22

To prevent overspray from creating grit when I repainted the repairs, I masked the wings with Post-it notes. The notes have low-tack adhesive, which is great for quick jobs like this.

23

I airbrushed light gull gray for the touch-ups, keeping the pressure at 15 psi to avoid lifting the Post-it notes.

24

While the brush was loaded with light gull gray, I airbrushed the spinner, gear doors, and outer wheel hubs on the sprues.

25 I cut the wheels from the sprues and removed mold seams from the tires. To mask the hubs, I applied tape, burnished it into the recesses with a toothpick, and then cut around it with a new No. 11 blade.

26 Pulling away the excess tape leaves a neatly masked hub that readies the tire for painting.

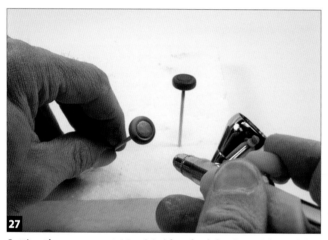

27 Setting the pressure at 15 psi, I airbrushed the tires with Model Master panzer grey (No. 1950). Keeping the pressure down minimizes the risk of paint being forced under the tape.

28 Then I sprayed just the sides of the tires with Model Master schwarzgrau RLM 66. The subtle difference between the sides and tread mimics the effect of wear on tires.

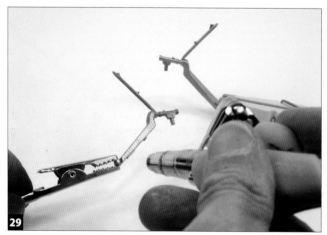

29 Working on the details, I airbrushed the main gear legs with Model Master aluminum. I separated them from the sprues, so I could easily clean the parts.

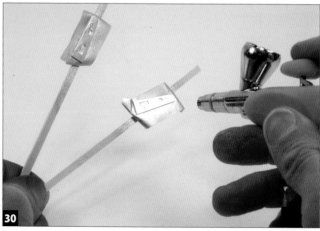

30 I loaded the brush with Model Master chrome silver (No. 1790) and sprayed the inside of the landing gear doors. I used tape to mask the outside surface.

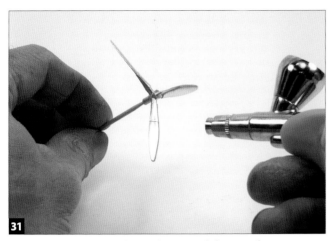

31 I also sprayed the propeller with a coat of chrome silver.

32 In preparation for applying decals, I misted Testors Glosscote (No. 1161) mixed with Testors lacquer thinner over the model at 20 psi.

33 Work slowly and build up the Testors Glosscote in multiple layers to produce a glass-smooth surface.

34 Microscale Micro Set and Micro Sol help settle the decals into the recessed panel lines.

35 While fixing a tear in the serial number decal, I scratched the paint with a hobby knife. By smoothing out the spot with 600-grit sandpaper, I limited the effect to the damaged spot.

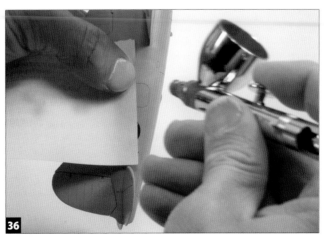

36 Holding a piece of paper over the decal, I touched up the spot with light gull gray sprayed at 15 psi.

37 I sealed the decals with Testors Glosscote sprayed at 20 psi. I could have applied the Glosscote over the entire model, but because the Buffalo had so few markings, I just used it on the decals.

38 After mixing burnt umber artist's oils with Turpenoid, I flowed the wash into the panel lines.

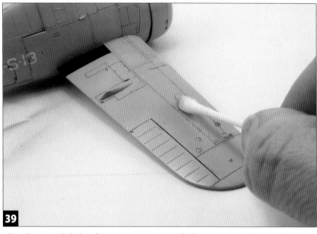

39 I let the model dry for 20 minutes and then wiped the wash with a dry cotton swab, which left the color in the recesses. Any streaking looks like excess fluid on the surface.

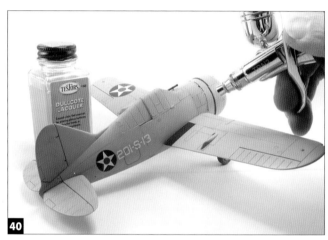

40 A coat of Testors Dullcote (No. 1160) muted the shine and blended the layers to tie the model together.

41 I scored the edges of the masks by running the tip of a new No. 11 blade along them, which lessened the chance of paint pulling off the surrounding frame.

42 Using tweezers to pull the mask back over the surface minimized the chance of damaging the canopy.

Post-shading for a dramatic result

So far, we've been talking about how to airbrush a nice smooth, even coat of color. But, the truth is, monochromatic camouflage, such as that on the Sherman in project 1, can look kind of boring—and even appear a little unrealistic. If you look at a full-size tank or aircraft, you'll see variations in the shade caused by the way light plays on the surface or by weathering. Post-shading mimics these effects with lighter or darker layers sprayed onto parts of the model. There are many ways to employ post-shading. I'm going to use Trumpeter's 1/35 scale Grizzly AVGP, a Canadian six-wheeled armored fighting vehicle, to demonstrate one common approach: spraying lighter shades in panel centers.

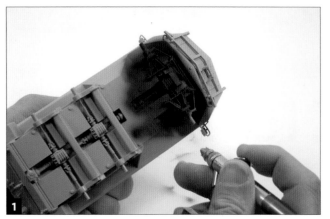

1 Using a single-action airbrush, I sprayed the model with a mix of 2 parts Tamiya acrylic olive green (XF-58) and 1 part Tamiya acrylic thinner. With the pressure set at 12 psi, I started spraying underneath, turning the model this way and that, so the entire complex suspension was covered.

2 Happy with the details, I dialed the pressure up to 20 psi and finished painting the Grizzly. Going back over the same areas a few times built up the color density to a nice even finish.

3 Post-shading means applying shades of the same color, so you can work fast. I removed the paint jar and flushed the airbrush with a little thinner to make sure any paint hadn't dried in it. Then I mixed a few drops of Tamiya J.N. grey (XF-12) to the olive green in the bottle to create a lighter shade of green. Avoid using straight white to lighten a shade as it can make the color look chalky.

4 I added more thinner to the paint. The post-shading mix should be a little thinner than paint used for normal coverage because you'll build up the effect in layers. After attaching the bottle to the brush, I set the pressure at about 12 psi. Thinner paint and lower pressure produces thin paint layers.

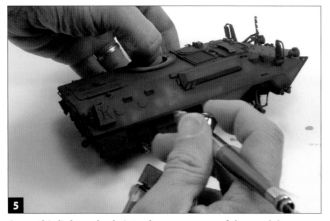

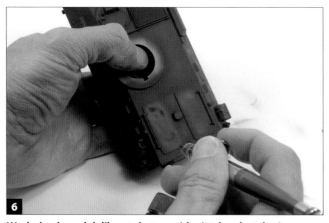

5 Spray this lighter shade into the open areas of the model, avoiding edges and panel lines. Start in the panel centers and work out toward the edge. This puts the heaviest layers near the center and feathers the effect to the edges.

6 Work slowly and deliberately to avoid mistakes, but don't worry too much if you color outside the lines. The thin paint makes minor slipups less obvious—and unevenness can add to the overall fading effect.

7 Before finishing the painting session, I lightened the olive green a little more with a few drops of J.N. grey. There's no science to this—add what seems right. You can always darken the shade with a few drops of olive green.

8 I sprayed the lightest shade into the panel centers. As a variation on this approach, think about limiting the lightest or brightest shades to the upper surfaces of the model. Darker, more muted tones are used on lower surfaces. This effect is often referred to as *color modulation* and mimics the way light falls on an object.

9 Here's my Grizzly after painting and post-shading. If you think the finish looks too stark after painting, you can mist the entire model with unaltered base color to tone mute the contrast. I didn't do it on the Grizzly, but when necessary, I thin the paint 60–70 percent and set the pressure at 15 psi. With the brush about 5" from the surface, I'll spray light, quick passes and stop when I'm satisfied with the effect.

10 In preparation for decals and weathering, I sealed the paint with clear gloss—in this case, Pledge FloorCare Multi-Surface Finish (formerly known as Future). It can be tricky to learn, though. I airbrush it straight from the bottle with the pressure at 15 psi. The first few passes are just mist coats to wet the surface.

11 More passes build up the layers and the shine. Keep the brush moving because the thin liquid can easily form runs and drips. Designed for vinyl floors, this clear acrylic dries smooth and doesn't react with most paints.

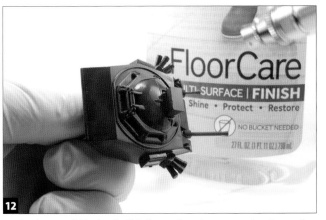

12 As the layers of Pledge build, the surface becomes glossier and glossier. It takes time, but the stuff is inexpensive and forms a barrier between the paint and potentially aggressive weathering products.

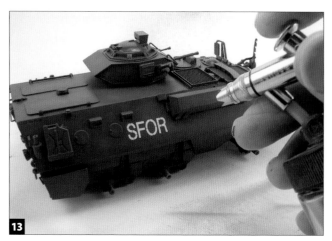

13 After applying the decals, I sealed them with another layer of Pledge.

14 Next, I added a wash of dark brown artist's oils to deepen shadows and emphasize panel lines and recesses. I sprayed the entire model with Acrylicos Vallejo matte varnish. Then I dry-brushed a 50:50 mix of olive green and J.N. grey to highlight raised detail and edges.

15 Out of the box, Trumpeter's soft vinyl tires are shiny—like they've just been coated with Armor All. They need to be dulled for realism. First, I roughed them up with a coarse sanding stick.

16 After mounting the tires on the wheels, I sprayed them with Vallejo matte varnish, which dulled any shine left after sanding.

17 I added a layer of road grime and dust to the Grizzly by spraying it with thin layers of Tamiya flat earth (XF-52) and desert yellow (XF-59). The mix for these layers is 20 percent paint, 40 percent clear flat, and 40 percent thinner. I hit the lower reaches of the vehicle and then the tires especially hard.

18 To give the tires a well-used look, I dry-brushed them with Tamiya German gray (XF-63). This colored the tread blocks but left the dirt color in the grooves and creases. Perfect!

Pre-shading monochromatic finishes

In addition to post-shading, you can pre-paint surfaces under the primary shade. This creates tonal variation in the colors and gives finishes drama. This can mimic the fading and variation often seen on full-size vehicles. Although I tend to lean on post-shading, I've pre-shaded and find it especially effective on the lighter gray camouflages commonly worn by modern fighters. Post-shading tends to wash out on light shades, so starting with a darker base followed by lighter shades works wonders. I used pre-shading on Trumpeter's 1/48 scale MiG-23M, and it would also work on F-16s, F-18s, and F-15s, as well as on Rafales and Eurofighters. You could also use it on lighter colored armor such as a desert-camouflaged Abrams tank or a winter-whitewashed KV-1.

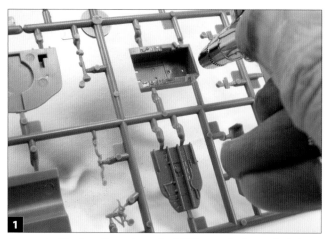

1

As usual with aircraft, work on the MiG began in the cockpit. I airbrushed the tub and walls with Model Master interior blue-green to match the unique Soviet cockpit color.

2

The engine gets sandwiched into the fuselage, so I painted the intakes medium gray and the jet pipe Testors Metalizer burnt iron. The jet pipe is molded in a single piece, so I dialed the pressure down to about 12 psi and carefully worked the brush around the interior from both ends.

3

Finding good matches for Soviet and Russian paints has been difficult in the past, but I discovered Akan paints while I was building the MiG. This Russian company specializes in Eastern Bloc camo colors, so I used their acrylics for the exterior, starting with the interior blue-green on the canopy frame.

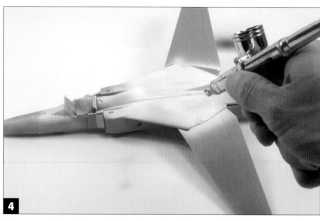

4

To ensure the Akan paints stayed on the model, I first sprayed on Vallejo acrylic primer. I used white instead of the usual gray to increase the contrast with the pre-shading to come. After the primer dried, I buffed the surface with 1500-grit sandpaper to remove any rough spots.

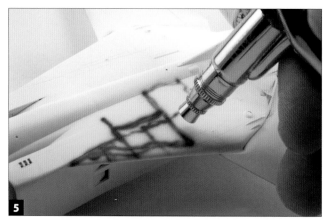

5

Akan's acrylics airbrush OK straight from the bottle, but they flow better with just a little thinner. You can add distilled water, Testors Universal Acrylic Thinner, or, as I did, Tamiya acrylic thinner. To start pre-shading, I airbrushed thin lines of Akan black along panel lines and around vents at 15 psi.

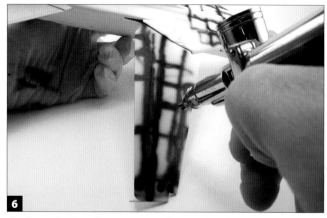

6

I built up the lines heavier around control surfaces and spoilers. It doesn't need to be perfect, so don't worry if you color outside the lines. It takes time and patience to do pre-shading right.

7

The rear fuselage, in particular the area adjacent to the exhaust, gets dirty. To show this, I airbrushed a concentration of black around the exhaust.

8

Right now, the paint looks something like a dog's breakfast, but it'll get better. The lines vary in width and density, which will add more diversity to the finished model's appearance so it doesn't look as uniform.

9

I mixed Akan gray (No. 73059) with a little Tamiya thinner to spray the camouflage layer. Starting in the middle of a panel, I worked the color out to, but not over, the black panel lines. Again, you don't need to cover the area in an even layer of color, as a varied density helps the finished appearance.

10

Move from panel to panel, leaving the black borders intact. We'll come back to those after all the panels are filled in. To maintain better control of the paint, I kept the pressure at 15 psi when doing this.

11

Once all the panels were painted, it was time to blend the pre-shading into the surface. Keeping the pressure at 15 psi, I widened the pattern a little and sprayed light coats over the panel lines.

12

The paint's density determines how many passes are needed to cover the black. Akan's paints seemed to cover pretty well. Notice the difference a single pass made from photo 11 to this one.

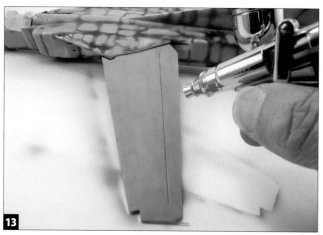

13 The goal is to all but eliminate the black paint, leaving just an impression of it under the gray. There's no set standard—just spray until you're happy with the result.

14 MiG-23 have radomes in the nose, tail, wing leading edges, and ventral fin. Masking most of them with Tamiya tape was easy, but the nose's compound curves presented a bit of a challenge. I started with a thin strip of tape that I could easily stretch and manipulate into place.

15 I airbrushed the radomes with Akan radio transparent grey (No. 73010) at 15 psi, starting along the edges of the tape.

16 I airbrushed the landing gear legs with Tamiya flat aluminum. A subsequent wash of dark brown artist's oils enhanced the molded detail and gave the legs a used look.

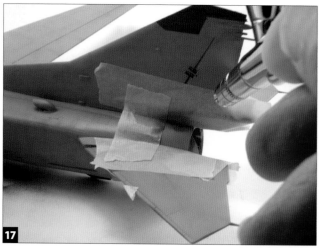

17 The MiG's rear fuselage features some natural-metal panels, so I masked the area and airbrushed Testors Metalizer burnt metal at 12 psi.

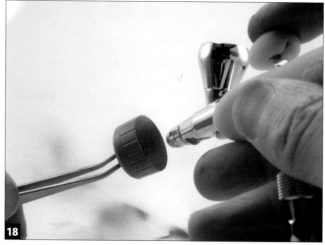

18 Before decaling and final assembly, I sprayed the exhaust section with Testors Metalizer burnt iron. This is a one-piece ring, so I carefully sprayed it inside and out.

Masking straight lines with tape

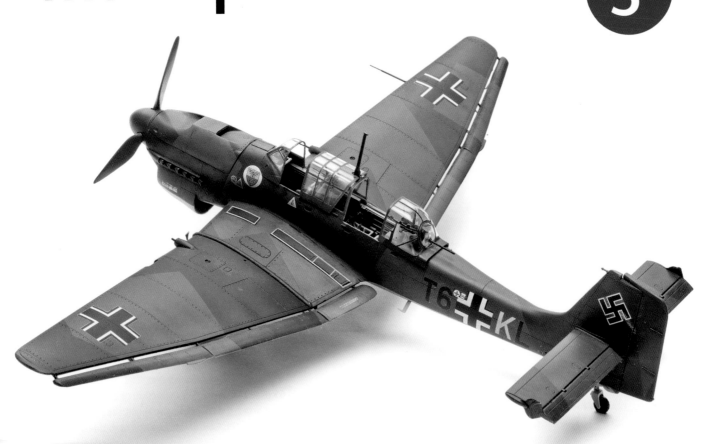

T he simplest things to mask are hard-edged, straight lines. Masking tape comes in rolls, and it's easy to pull off a piece and lay it along the line to be masked. That makes masking boot stripes on ships, cheat lines on airliners, and demarcations between upper and lower surfaces a snap. It gets a little more complicated when you mask hard-edged splinter camouflage like that used on World War II Luftwaffe bombers and early fighters. I built Italeri's Ju 87B-1 Stuka based in France in 1940 wearing the classic scheme of RLM 70 schwarzgrun and RLM 71 olivgrun over RLM 65 hellblau.

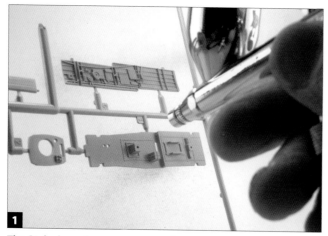

1

The Stuka has a long canopy over its two-seat cockpit, so it pays to spend a little extra time painting and detailing the cockpit. I started by airbrushing Testors Model Master Acryl RLM 02 grau over the cockpit walls and floor. I kept the pressure at 15 psi to avoid flooding the surface but yet reaching the corners.

2

Italeri includes a photoetched-metal instrument panel and insert, which I painted RLM 02 at the same time as the rest of the cockpit. The acrylic paint can chip when the metal is flexed, so handle the pieces with care after painting.

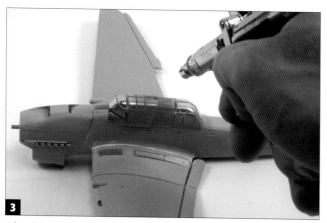

3

After hand-painting the rest of the cockpit details and assembling the model, I masked the canopy with Bare-Metal Foil. I sprayed the frames with Mr. Hobby Mr. Color RLM 02 (No. 60) to match the interior. I used these lacquers for all of the exterior painting, mixing them with equal parts Mr. Color Leveling Thinner.

4

I sprayed RLM 65 (No. 115) over the underside of the aircraft, starting under and around details like the dive brakes and bomb racks. Properly thinned, Mr. Color lacquers airbrush beautifully at 20 psi. You'll know very quickly if the paint is too thick because cobweb-like tendrils will form around edges and corners.

5

I widened the pattern to spray larger expanses such as the wings and belly of the plane. Make sure you spray the paint far enough up the sides of the plane so that it meets the upper surface camouflage.

6

Once the blue was on and dry, I masked the lower surfaces. I laid a strip of 6mm Tamiya masking tape along the demarcation line of the rear fuselage, holding one end in place with my thumb. As I pulled the tape into place, I slid my thumb along it to press it into place and to seal the edge.

7 The camouflage wraps around the leading edge of the wings. I marked the edge of the color with a thin strip of tape, pressing it around details like the ridge at the wing bend. Wider tape (14mm) backed the edge. I paid attention to raised spots like the dive brakes. Note the short piece of tape masking the chin scoop.

8 To start the upper surface camouflage, I sprayed RLM 71 dunkel-grun (No. 17) along the masked edges under the wings at 20 psi.

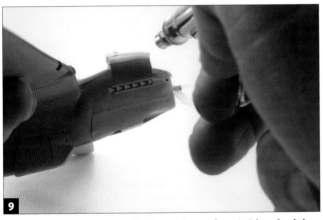

9 Keeping the brush perpendicular to the surface, I airbrushed the masked edges of the cowl and chin.

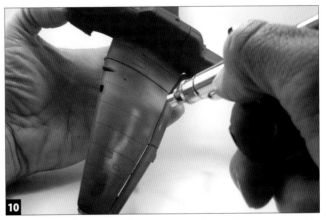

10 With all the edges painted, I opened up the pattern and sprayed the entire upper surface of the Stuka with RLM 71. I didn't mask the rear edges of the wings, preferring instead to spray straight down past the trailing surfaces. This left a hard edge without the risk of tape pulling up any paint.

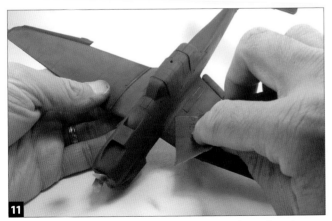

11 Small vortices of paint generated by the airbrush produced a slightly rough texture on the paint around the wing roots. Fine sandpaper and a gentle touch smoothed the area without damaging the paint on the plastic, but some paint eroded from the photoetched-brass walkways.

12 The key to getting a sharp angle on splinter patterns is to miter the tape at the corners. I placed strips of Tamiya tape on a glass plate and then sliced them in half at roughly a 45 degree angle.

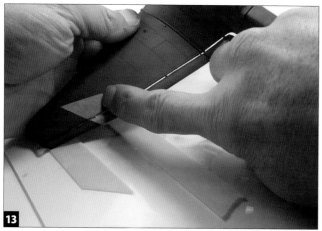

13 I placed the pointed angle of the tape at the spot on the model where the corner of the shape needed to be, and aligned the edge with the outline of the pattern being masked. Light finger pressure is all that's need to seal the mask.

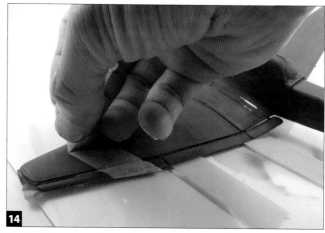

14 To start the next edge, I aligned the tip from another angled piece of tape with the point of the one on the model, and then laid the tape along the edge of the area being masked. To locate these edges, match features on the model with the drawings.

15 After outlining the shape, I filled the interior with a scrap of tape. It may be necessary, as seen here, to cut a point into the tape to match the shape.

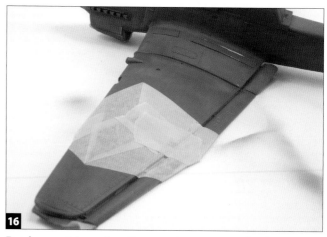

16 For sharp points, such as those on the upper rear fuselage, I cut points into thin strips of Tamiya tape. I placed these so that the tip corresponded with the points seen in the diagrams. If necessary, I backfilled the area with more tape.

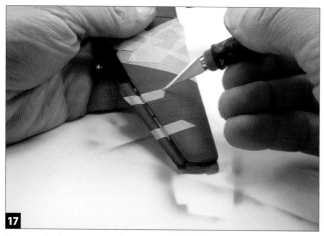

17 If you misplace a strip of tape, gently slide the tip of a No. 11 blade under a corner and pry it off the model. Keep the blade parallel to the surface to avoid gouging the paint.

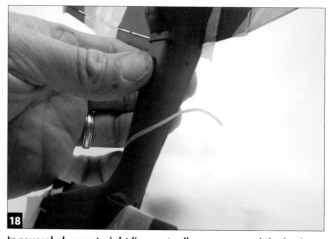

18 In several places, straight lines actually curve around the body of the plane. I cut a strip of tape just a few millimeters wide and drew it around the model, stretching and bending it to produce a straight line when seen on the model.

19 The Stuka is ready for paint, although covered in tape as it is, it looks more suited for the emergency room.

20 I started the layer of RLM 70 (No. 18) by spraying it along the edges of the tape at 20 psi. Once the edges of an area were painted, I filled in the interior, working slowly to ensure proper coverage and density.

21 The moment of truth came when I peeled the tape slowly back against the surface of the model. This keeps the pressure on the painted surface low and minimizes damage. The tape pulled paint off the Bare-Metal Foil masks on the canopy and on the walkways, but there was no damage to the plastic areas.

22 One of my favorite moments in painting is when multiple layers of masking come off and the finished camouflage is revealed. It's even better when it turns out the way you planned.

23 The tape did pull paint up in a couple of spots under the airplane. I touched them up with a little RLM 65 at 15 psi.

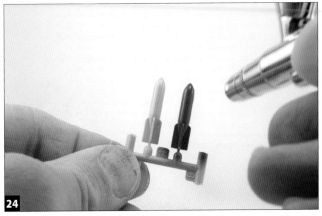

24 To paint the ordnance, I trimmed the sprue attachment points from the sides of the 50-pound bombs and smoothed them with a sanding stick. I left them attached to the sprue at the aft end for easier painting. That spot was easy to touch up after removing the sprue.

Painting small-scale ships

Working with 1/700 scale waterline ship models often means painting just three or four colors. But that doesn't mean there weren't challenges. I built Aoshima's Japanese light cruiser *Kitakami*, and these techniques will work for any single-color waterline ship. I built the model in subassemblies including the hull and superstructures that would be the same color as the deck and hull. I left the other structures separate.

1 Before painting, I cleaned the surface with Testors Plastic Prep. Applying it with a cotton swab makes it easy to get into tight spots such as the gun tubs.

2 You can paint the hull first and then the deck, or, as I did, the deck first and then the hull. I sprayed Tamiya linoleum deck brown over the forward deck.

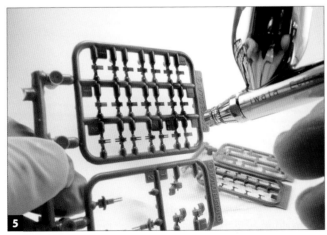

3 As I sprayed, I moved the model and airbrush around so that fixtures like the corners of the gun tubs and the superstructure received an even coat of paint. I kept the pressure at 20 psi.

4 While the deck dried, I sprayed details that remained on the sprues. I started with Tamiya flat black (XF-1) on the mini submarines that would be mounted on the rear deck.

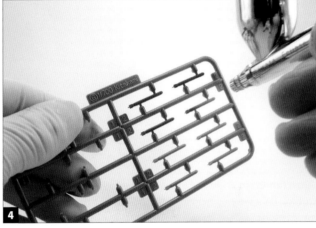

5 I emptied the excess flat black from the airbrush reservoir. I then added a few drops of Tamiya gun metal (X-10) and painted the ship's antiaircraft guns.

6 Before painting the hull, you need to mask the deck. I cut Tamiya tape into ¼" x ¹⁄₁₆" strips and placed them around the features on the deck.

7 I transferred the strips to the model with the tip of a No. 11 blade and positioned them on the model with the help of a toothpick.

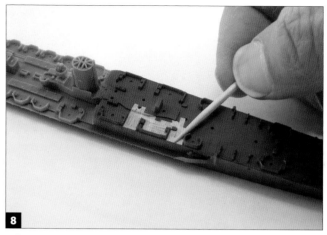

8 I also used the toothpick to burnish each tape strip against the surface.

9 When fitting strips around a feature, overlap them to cover the surface. It's a time-consuming method but one that produces good results.

10 To fit tight spots, you'll need to trim some strips shorter.

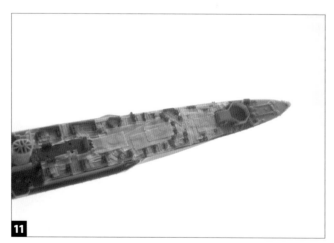

11 After masking around the features, use larger pieces of tape to cover the wider expanses until the entire deck is completely masked. Then the hull is ready to paint.

12 I mixed Tamiya IJN Kure Arsenal gray (XF-75) with thinner and began airbrushing the model, starting with the deck fittings.

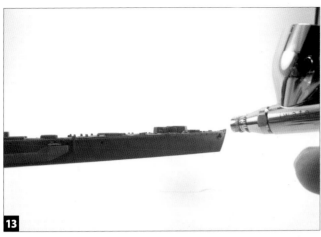

13 Move the ship around in order to cover every surface. Vertical surfaces like the superstructure and gun tubs are best painted from a low angle.

14 Next, I painted the rear hull and deck, keeping the pressure low to be able to work close and avoid overspray and excess paint.

15 Attaching the built-up superstructure sections to wooden stir sticks with poster putty makes moving and painting them easy.

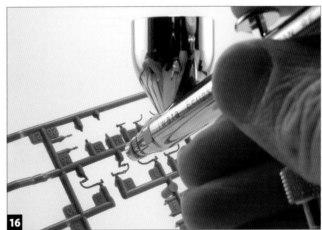

16 There are many small details on ships that are best painted before being attached to the model. I airbrushed those parts with Kure Arsenal gray.

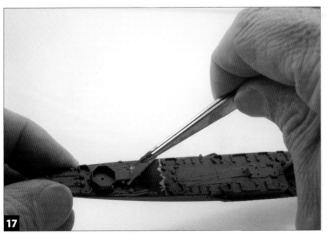

17 I lifted a corner of a deck mask with tweezers and peeled it off the model. Use the tip of the knife or a toothpick to carefully lift stubborn bits of tape.

18 Once the tape is off, a neatly edged deck is revealed. With so many corners, nooks, and crannies, you will inevitably find a few mistakes, but they are easy to correct with hand-brushing.

19

As on many ships, *Kitakami*'s funnels are topped by a section of black. I edged the area with thin, easily manipulated strips of tape, maneuvering them around the stack and pipes with tweezers.

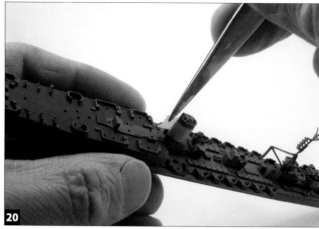

20

I finished masking the funnels with larger pieces of tape, pressing the tape in place with a round toothpick.

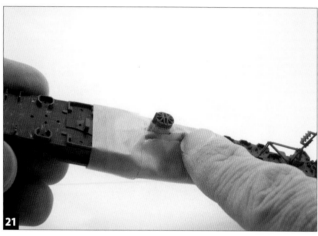

21

For the funnel already installed on the model, I protected the surrounding details with more tape, lightly secured and not forced into place.

22

I sprayed the funnels Tamiya flat black with the pressure dialed down to 12 psi to minimize the chance of paint being pushed past the tape.

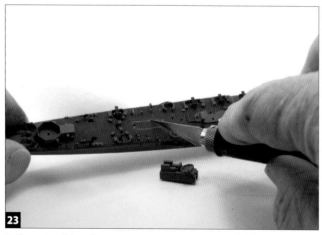

23

Before attaching the superstructure sections and other larger components, I scraped paint from the mating surfaces to assure a good bond for the glue. Work carefully and check your progress so as not to mar the surrounding deck.

24

Once all of the details and subassemblies were attached, I sprayed the model with Tamiya clear flat (XF-86) to dull any shine from the glue and to blend touch-ups. The little Japanese cruiser is now ready for the high seas.

Achieving perfect gloss for cars

Gloss finishes are a challenge. Flat paints seem to spray easily and provide a smooth surface, whereas gloss paint is touchy and inclined to look uneven. A bad gloss finish can make a scale model look like a toy. The keys to airbrushing realistic gloss finishes are surface preparation and finishing work. I built an old Revell 1/24 scale Ferrari 308, one of my favorite cars because of its association with *Magnum, P.I.,* one of my favorite TV shows. The kit went together well enough, but the 35-year-old, red plastic started to show its age, with surface imperfections and flash. I wanted to use Tamiya Italian red for the classic Ferrari, but it was only available in a spray can, so I needed to decant the paint and primer in order to airbrush the car.

1 When you need a color that's only available in a spray can, but you want to apply it with the speed and accuracy of an airbrush, you need to decant it. The first step is cutting a drinking straw to 4–5 inches long. The flexible kind, like I'm using here, is ideal.

2 Tape the straw over the nozzle of the spray can, making the fit as tight as possible. Make sure it's secure because, if it comes off during the decanting process, you'll end up wearing most of the color.

3 Prepare a receptacle for the paint. I use a jar or bottle with a lid that can be closed, especially if I need to store the paint for a length of time. Secure aluminum foil over the opening with a rubber band. Make sure the paint won't attack the container, such as a styrene foam cup (don't ask me how I know).

4 Shake the can vigorously before spraying to ensure that the decanted color (or primer, in this case) is properly mixed. You won't want to shake it after spraying because any paint left in the straw will go all over.

5 Insert the straw through a hole in the foil and depress the button on the spray can. Paint will flow into the container. Continue spraying until you have enough paint to complete the job.

6 Cover the bottle to keep dust and grit from falling into it, but don't—and I mean do not—seal it. Let the container sit for several hours, so the propellant in the paint can gas off. If you try to use it, or even mix it now, the results can be messy or, worse, cause damage to your airbrush.

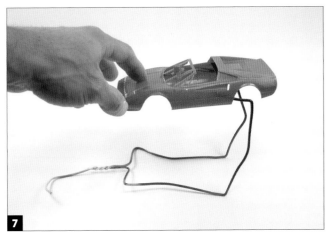

7 In preparation for painting, I suspended the Ferrari's body on a stand made from an old wire coat hanger.

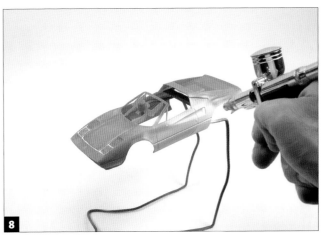

8 I started spraying the primer in the recessed details of the car, including the door outlines, air scoops, and vents. I find spraying Tamiya primer works best at 30–35 psi, so remember to keep the brush moving to prevent runs or excess paint.

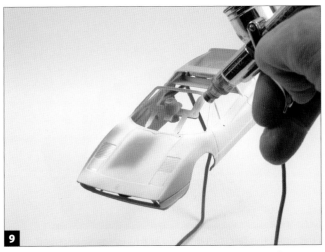

9 With details primed, I moved on to cover wider areas such as the hood, err, trunk lid. I left the sprue in the windshield during painting and while handling to avoid damaging the fragile frame.

10 Although I glued the engine hatch closed, some parts of the compartment will be visible underneath the car. I airbrushed primer into these areas to aid the coverage and adhesion of subsequent colors.

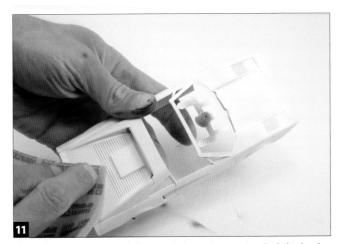

11 The primer came out a little rough in spots, so I sanded the body with a 600-grit pad from Tamiya.

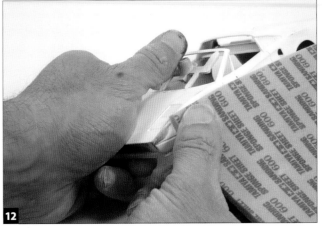

12 Doing its job, the primer revealed a few imperfections including mold seams along the sides of the car and a few sink marks in the doors. To fix, I sanded the mold seams and filled the sink marks with a little super glue.

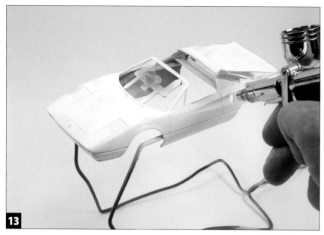

13 I sprayed on another layer of primer to check the body work and to provide an even surface for the red paint. You may need to repeat this process several times, but the extra work now can save you heartache later.

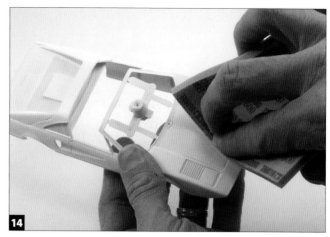

14 To make sure the surface was smooth and even, more sanding followed the final primer coat. Again, be patient and take the extra steps here for the payoff later in the process.

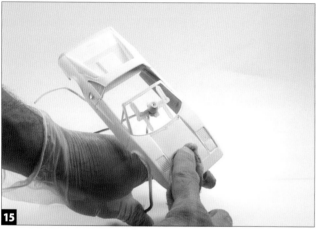

15 Before moving on to the color coats, I rubbed the surface with a tack cloth to remove any dust or sanding debris that would mar the paint and result in a rough surface.

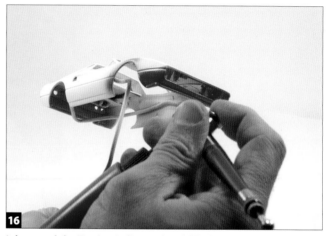

16 I decanted the Tamiya Italian red and filled the siphon-feed bottle on my single-action airbrush. I started spraying the color in hard-to-reach areas, such as the front spoiler and wheel wells, keeping the pressure at about 30 psi and the airbrush moving.

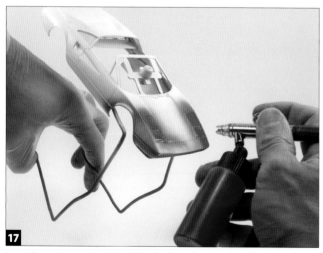

17 I continued spraying details including the vents and recessed headlight covers. Airbrushing these tight spots first assures better coverage, even if you want to finish with a spray can, as many car modelers do.

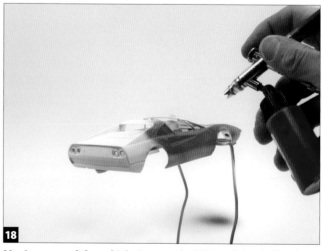

18 Moving around the vehicle, I sprayed additional details like the window louvers and door outlines. This coat maintains the density of these spots when you begin painting the overall color.

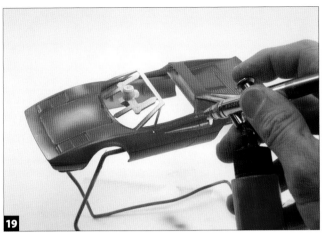

19 Don't rush the process and give these recesses two or three light passes. Work until you are satisfied that all the details are adequately covered.

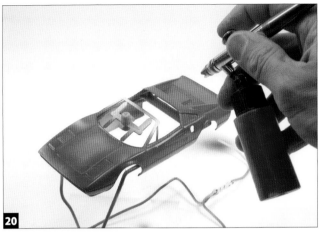

20 Then, you can begin spraying the overall coats. I adjusted the setscrew on the airbrush to widen the pattern. The first pass over the model should cover it with a light coat that doesn't completely obscure the plastic.

21 The next series of passes should cover the plastic, but they may appear a little rough in places. Don't worry, the next layer will take care of that.

22 Referred to as *wet coats*, the last passes should lay down a heavy layer of paint that covers the surface and leaves the model glossy. The secret here is to move the brush enough to prevent problems but keep it moving slow so the paint builds up nicely.

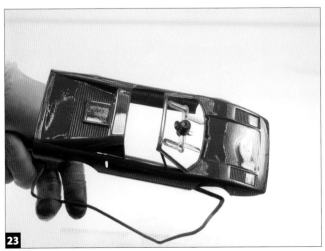

23 The Ferrari's looking pretty good here, with a nice reflection of the overhead light in the hood. There's a fine line between just enough paint and too much, so it pays to practice this technique.

24 No matter how carefully I cover a model after painting, a bit of lint or dust always ends up in the color. Here, I sand it out of the paint with 1500-grit paper. Work in small circles in the area of the blemish to minimize any damage.

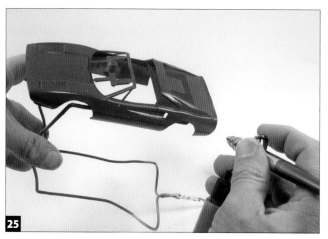

25

Next, I repainted the model using the same three steps to ensure proper coverage. You can try spraying just the affected area, but when doing so, sometimes the edges of the spray pattern end up being a little rough. It's often better to just bite the bullet and spray the whole thing. There are no shortcuts to producing a good gloss finish.

26

To prepare for a layer of clear gloss, I buffed the entire model with 1500-grit sandpaper to smooth out any rough spots that might cause problems later.

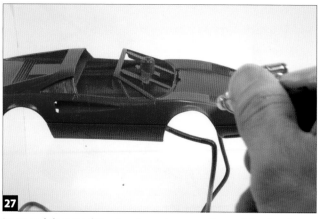

27

I sprayed decanted Tamiya clear gloss over the car's body using the same three-step process: a mist coat, a heavier coat for coverage, and a final wet coat for gloss.

28

Magnum's ride looks pretty good under eight or nine coats of primer, paint, and clear coat, but it can be even better after buffing.

29

I started by carefully sanding the entire surface with Tamiya 1500-grit paper, taking it right up to the edge of details. Be careful around ridges, such as the rear edge of the engine cover. Sanding across it too many times will reveal the white primer and necessitate touch-up painting.

30

To properly finish a car, you'll need graduated sanding pads or cloths. These usually come in sets with grits from 1800 or 3200 up to 12000. The bigger the number, the finer the grit.

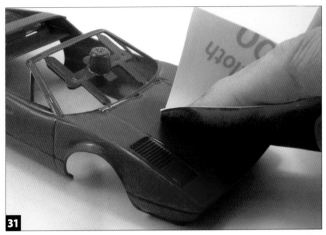

31 Starting with the coarsest pad or cloth, in this case 3200, I gently buffed every surface on the car's body. It's important to work through the set one cloth at a time without skipping any. It may seem a shame to spoil the shine, but the results are worthwhile.

32 By the time you get to the second last finishing cloth, the shine is returning. Notice how sharp the reflection of the bulb and reflector from my photo booth looks. This is a good measure of progress. Ideally, any reflections should be perfect.

33 Finished for now, I prepared the surface for trim painting and final assembly. The final step in the process is a light rubdown with Novus No. 2 Plastic Polish, but I do that after everything else to minimize the amount of handling the model receives, which could mar the finish.

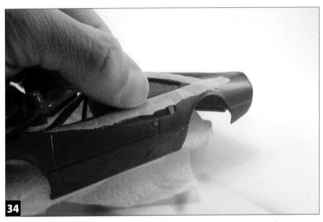

34 The Ferrari 308 has several areas that need to be painted semigloss black including the windshield frame and the louvers behind the seats, so I masked the flowing lines with thin strip of Tamiya tape.

35 The louvered panels end with curves. I laid tape across the corners and then carefully traced around the molded detail with a No. 11 blade. Use a new blade for this, so you don't need to press hard to slice through the paper. This minimizes damage to the paint underneath.

36 Large pieces of tape applied only to the edging strips back the masking and protect against overspray. I wanted to minimize the tape's contact with the surface in order to avoid damaging the smoothed, buffed paint.

37 I airbrushed decanted Tamiya semigloss black over the trim. The paint is thin and airbrush-ready, so I sprayed it at 12 psi to minimize overspray. A few passes did the trick in most spots.

38 Some of the trim, like the bumpers and dashboard, are separate. I taped them to a piece of cardboard and airbrushed them.

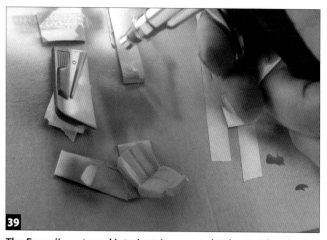

39 The Ferrari's seats and interior trim are tan leather. I airbrushed them with Tamiya desert yellow acrylic at 20 psi.

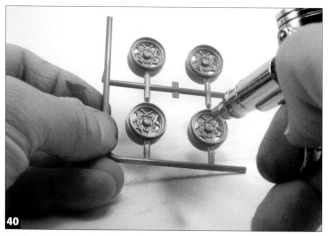

40 I airbrushed the wheels with Testors German metallic silver enamel to match the 308's brushed alloy rims. There are a lot of tight recesses and overhangs on the wheels, and it took several coats to cover the red plastic.

41 Back to the body. The black trim overlaps, so I painted it in stages. The long stripe on the side was easy to mask with long strips of Tamiya tape. I airbrushed it with decanted Tamiya semigloss black at 12 psi.

42 Finally, I masked the floor and footwell that I'd previously painted tan, and then airbrushed the center console and back wall semigloss black.

Cutting tape masks

Nothing produces a sharp-edged masked line better than tape. It's easy to use when lines are straight. You just pull it off the roll and apply it to the surface. But what if the subject has a paint scheme marked by curves, such as a Royal Air Force fighter? Cutting tape to shape off the model makes the job easy. I built Hasegawa's Spitfire Mk.Vb in standard RAF temperate colors. As a twist, this aircraft has white ID stripes for an operation against the German-occupied French port of Dieppe.

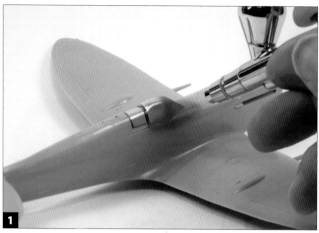

1

I masked the canopy with Bare-Metal Foil and then sprayed the frames with Acrylicos Vallejo Model Air pale green (No. 71.095). These paints are designed to be airbrushed straight from the bottle, but I find adding several drops of Vallejo Airbrush Thinner (No. 71.061) keeps them flowing.

2

After wiping the model with rubbing alcohol to remove oils, I sprayed it with Vallejo white primer (No. 73600). This tough coating promotes paint adhesion and reveals flaws. On this plane, it also became the white color for the stripes on the nose and tail.

3

Measuring the stripes found on the instructions and using a set of Xtradecal markings, I determined that the stripes would be about 5mm wide on the model. I applied Tamiya tape to a smooth surface and marked the width.

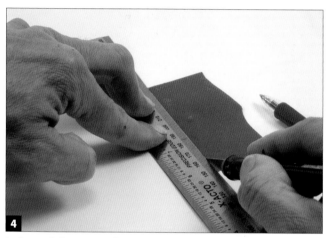

4

I trimmed the tape with a new No. 11 blade, using a metal straightedge as a guide.

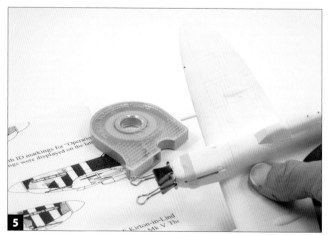

5

I placed the foremost stripe on the model, aligning it with the molded features, and then burnished it with a fingernail and toothpick for a tight seal.

6

Scoops and vents can interfere with the tape's lie, so I slit the tape with a knife and pressed the tape around the detail. I then used a small bit of tape to mask the raised detail.

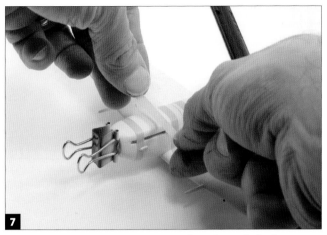

7 I masked the rearmost stripe next, and used it with the foremost stripe to position and consistently space the remaining stripes.

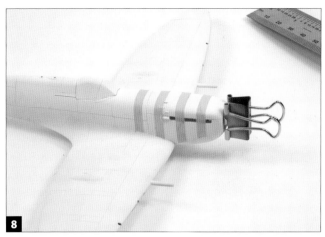

8 After fitting a brand new blade, I trimmed the ends of the tape along the panel lines where the stripes ended. The upper surfaces of the horizontal stabilizers received two stripes each.

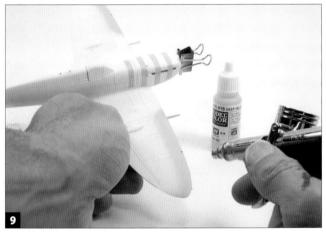

9 Before spraying the camouflage, I airbrushed the leading edges of the wing yellow. Yellow is a translucent color that will show underlying shades, so it's good practice to paint it over white.

10 I also airbrushed the sky band on the rear fuselage.

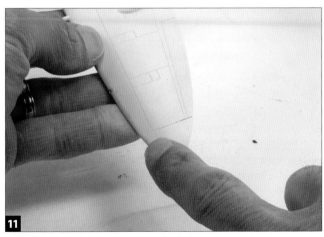

11 To mask the leading edges, I applied thin strips of Tamiya tape, which easily conformed to the curves. I also used thin strips to outline the tail band and then filled in with wider strips.

12 I made life easy and painted the Spitfire with Tamiya's RAF matched colors. Starting underneath, I sprayed medium sea gray 2 (XF-83) mixed with 35 percent Tamiya thinner at 25 psi. Then I added a few drops of flat white (XF-2) and post-shaded the panel centers at 15 psi.

13 I masked the lower sections with tape along the demarcation lines, burnishing with a fingernail to seal the edge. Applying tape under wings protects them from overspray, but most of the masking along the edges will be directional—holding the brush so paint doesn't go past a certain point.

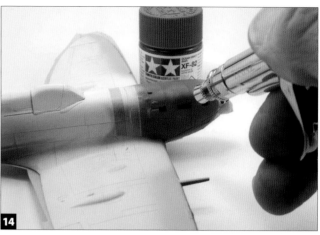

14 I cut ocean gray 2 (XF-82) with 35 percent Tamiya thinner, and then airbrushed it around the masked stripes at 15 psi to avoid lifting the tape.

15 Next, I moved on to the rest of the model, starting with the wing roots at 20 psi. I post-shaded panel centers by spraying ocean gray lightened with a few drops of white.

16 Using a photocopier, I enlarged the painting diagrams to 1/48 scale. To determine the ratio, I measured the airplane's length on the drawing and on the model. I divided the length of the model (6.9375") by the measurement from the drawing (4.25"). The result, 1.63, translated to a 163 percent enlargement.

17 The plan drawings required a different copy ratio. I covered the enlargements with clear packing tape.

18 I applied strips of Tamiya tape to cover the ocean gray areas of the drawing. You can use another type of tape as long as it is thin enough so you can see the drawing underneath.

19 Using a new No. 11 blade, I traced the outline of the gray area onto the masking tape. You only need to press hard enough to cut the masking tape and not through the packing tape or the paper.

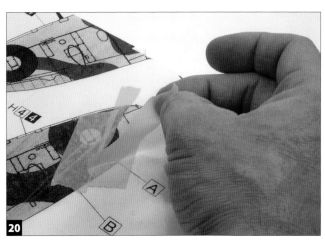

20 Pulling gently, I removed the mask from the drawing. Remember to cut past the edge of the drawing so the tape overlaps the model.

21 Referring to the drawing, I positioned the cut mask on the model.

22 The cannon bulges prevented the tape from conforming to the wing. I cut a slit along one side of the bulge, pushed the tape down, and then made up the shortfall with a little more tape.

23 I finished transferring everything I could see in the plan view and then moved to the sides. You can see a mismatch on the nose, probably the result of the distortion from the two-dimensional drawing to the model. I cut a curved section to smooth the line.

24 I encountered the opposite problem farther back, so I carefully trimmed the excess from the mask with a No. 11 blade. The blade needs to be sharp to go cleanly through the tape without having to use a lot of pressure, which could damage the paint.

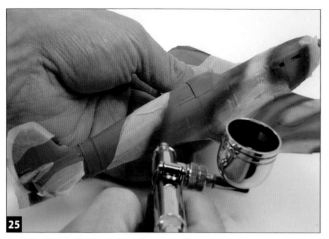

25 Satisfied with the position of the masks, I airbrushed the model dark green 2 (XF-81) mixed with 35 percent Tamiya thinner. I started by spraying along the tape edges at 15 psi, which helped seal the masks.

26 Then I turned the pressure up to 25 psi and filled in the larger areas between the masks. Once again, I post-shaded panel centers by adding a few drops of white to the mix.

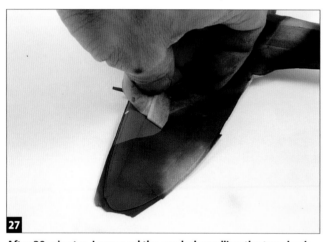

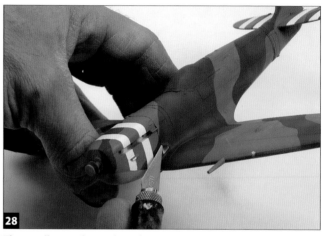

27 After 30 minutes, I removed the masks by pulling the tape back against the surface to minimize the risk of paint being pulled away. By grasping the sections overhanging the edges, I easily removed the large masks.

28 The smaller masks, such as the ID stripes, required a gentler approach. With the tip of a knife blade, I pried up one stripe's edge, so I could peel it off with a tweezers. I then added layers of clear gloss, decals, more clear gloss, washes, and clear flat.

29 I sprayed some small details, including the exhausts, on the sprue before attaching them to the model. Testors Metalizer burnt iron is a great base for exhausts.

30 Before attaching the exhausts, I airbrushed a mix of Tamiya clear flat and several drops of black back along the fuselage side. With the pressure at 15 psi, I started close to the surface where the exhausts were, pulling the nozzle away from the model as I quickly moved the brush aft.

Create soft edges with raised masks

PROJECT
9

Spraying soft lines is easy to do freehand, but it can be a problem keeping the lines straight. The secret is to mask the lines, but raise the edge of the tape or paper mask a bit. A little paint can go past the edge to produce a slightly soft edge. The height of the masked edge above the surface affects the sharpness of the demarcation. You can raise the tape with rolls of tape or poster putty. I used the former to paint Italeri's 1/48 scale Douglas SBD-5 in midwar, three-color camouflage. This scheme was used on most U.S. Navy aircraft during 1943 and 1944. This Dauntless is marked as an aircraft loaned by the Marines to the Royal New Zealand Air Force.

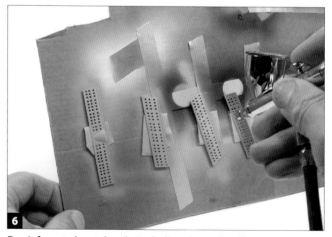

1 For the rear-most section, I applied tape to the inside surface and then stuck it to the cardboard.

2 I attached the windshield to the model and used the kit's optional closed canopy to mask the cockpit. Using small dots of white glue, I secured it for the duration. After painting, the glue can be softened with water for removal.

3 Before attaching the cowl to the airframe, I sprayed the inside surface with Model Master light ghost gray. Keeping the pressure low (12–15 psi) when airbrushing closed spaces such as this minimizes overspray and grit from vortices.

4 The Dauntless features unique perforated dive flaps. To build the model in landing configuration, I needed to paint these separate pieces off the model. I taped them to cardboard for easier handling.

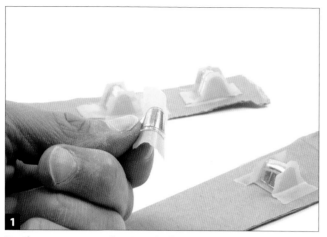

5 I primed the model with Model Master flat gull gray. In addition to revealing construction flaws, the light gray makes a good starting point for post-shading the airplane's white underside. I thinned the enamels with 1 part thinner to 2 parts paint.

6 Don't forget about details, including those dive flaps. It's so much easier to prime all of the components together.

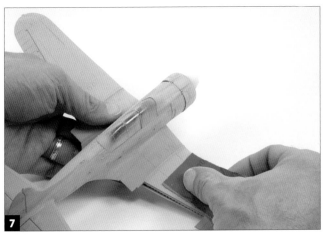

7 To ensure a smooth foundation for the colors to come, I lightly rubbed the primer coat with 2000-grit sandpaper. It doesn't take much sanding to remove any roughness in the finish, and it makes a big difference in the results.

8 I thinned some Model Master flat white and started spraying the panels' internal areas. I wasn't aiming for complete or uniform coverage, as minor variations add to the overall weathered effect.

9 Working at 15 psi, I continued spraying flat white between panel lines and details.

10 A misted overcoat of thin flat white softened the contrast and left the underside patchy white. I sprayed this layer at 15 psi.

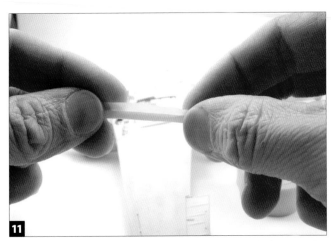

11 Next, I began masking lines on the aircraft. I first rolled strips of Tamiya masking tape into worms, with the sticky side out. They don't need to be tight because this is how they prop up the masks. I usually aim for a cylinder about ⅛" in diameter.

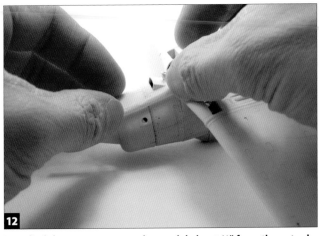

12 I applied the tape worms to the model about ⅛" from the actual line to be masked. If you place one too close to the line, it acts as a mask itself and produces a hard demarcation. If you place one too far away, it won't support the mask properly.

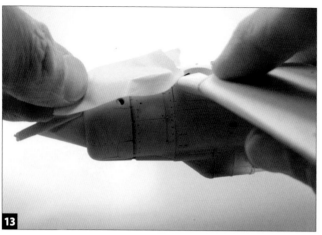

13

14

To make the masks, I stuck strips of tape to the rolls, and aligned an edge with the line to be masked. To secure a mask, press lightly to avoid smashing the tape roll and ruining the effect.

This photo shows the kind of gap you are looking for, with the tape being about ¹⁄₁₆" above the surface. Do your best to maintain a uniform separation so the softness of the color demarcation remains consistent.

15

16

Once the masking was complete, I airbrushed the fuselage sides and tail with Model Master intermediate blue (No. 1720), starting along the tape edges. With the pressure at 20 psi, I held the nozzle about 2" away from—and perpendicular—to the surface. The tape under the wing, adjacent to the fuselage, protects it from overspray.

A couple of steady passes should be all you need for coverage along the masking tape. Avoid spraying too much paint in these areas or you may produce an uneven line.

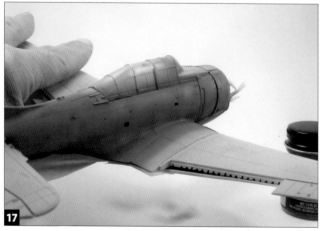

17

18

The South Pacific was rough on aircraft finishes, so I faded panel centers by adding a little flat white to the intermediate blue and applied it at 15 psi. Avoid spraying post-shading paint too close to the masks.

When I stripped off the masks, I saw that the masks worked—for the most part. While the rear fuselage looked good, the spot near the wing root showed overspray. I filled the brush with flat white and touched up the area freehand.

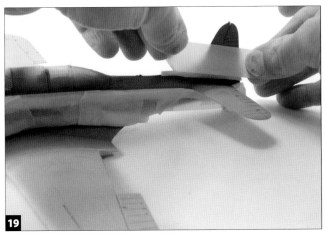

19 After lightly sanding the surface, I masked the intermediate blue sections with more rolls of tape and raised edges. I waited 48 hours between layers to ensure that the paint was properly cured before applying tape.

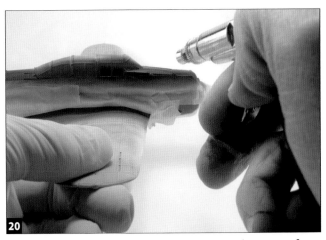

20 I started the flat sea blue (Model Master No. 1718) upper surfaces by spraying a couple of passes along the tape edge with the brush perpendicular to the surface. Don't spray the upper parts of the airframe yet.

21 Moving to an area as far from the masked edges as possible, I airbrushed the wings. Note the hazy sections of blue between the wing's tip and root. Static electricity attracts atomized paint. It's not too bad there, but some static electricity attracted blue paint on the white painted undersides, which was not so great.

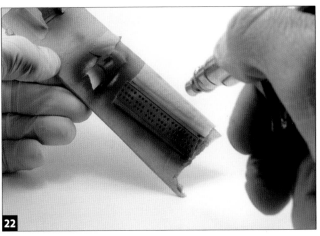

22 Staying away from the fuselage masks, I painted the canopy sections and upper dive brakes flat sea blue. I set the pressure to 15 psi to minimize the risk of paint bleeding past the tape.

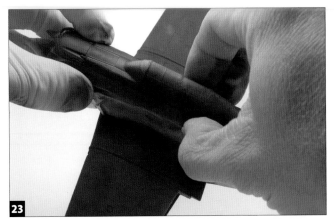

23 Twenty minutes after spraying initial passes along the tape, I returned to the fuselage. I lightly pressed the tape against the surface to prevent overspray ruining the sprayed demarcation line. This should prevent the problems I encountered between the white and intermediate blue.

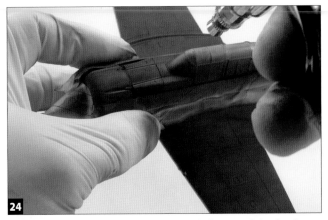

24 I dialed the pressure to 12 psi to airbrush the top of the fuselage. Too much pressure and the air will lift the tape and force paint under it. I carefully filled in the areas between the previously sprayed sections.

25 Before removing the masks, I mixed a little white into the sea blue and post-shaded the panels. In wartime photos, you see that this color faded considerably under the tropical sun, so I added more white than normal for post-shading. I set the pressure at 15 psi.

26 Here's the result after I removed the masks. I airbrushed a few touch-ups along the color separations, and left the model sit for several days before sealing the finish with Pledge FloorCare Multi-Surface Finish.

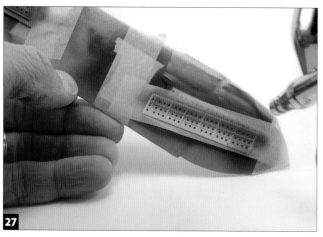

27 I flipped the dive brakes over to reveal the white painted interior surfaces and pressed them firmly against strips of tape. Airbrushing Model Master insignia red (No. 1705) at 15 psi gave the brakes their characteristic finish.

28 After applying the decals, I sealed them with another coat of Pledge, which acted as a foundation for weathering washes. A final coat of Tamiya clear flat unified the finish and gave the aircraft a prototypical wartime dull appearance.

29 I pressed the propeller onto the end of a toothpick, and airbrushed the tips with Model Master insignia yellow (No. 1708) at 15 psi. Also at 15 psi, I sprayed the hub cover Model Master chrome silver (No. 1790).

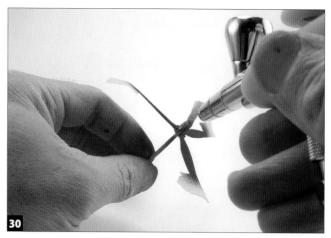

30 Tamiya masking tape protected the yellow tips and silver hub as I airbrushed the rest of the prop flat black (No. 1749). I also painted the landing gear, bomb, and exhausts before assembling and finishing the dive-bomber.

Silly Putty produces sharp camo

The first time I heard about using Silly Putty for masking I was incredulous. But it turns out that it's the perfect solution for masking odd shapes that require hard demarcations between colors. I've used it when camouflaging Royal Air Force aircraft and German armor. It's also useful for places such as aircraft wheel wells and automobile engine bays. You can push the sticky putty into corners and around details. It can be cut with scissors or a knife, and it adheres well enough to maintain position on the surface and form a seal, but it won't mar underlying paint or leave residue. It turned out to be a great choice to use for painting three-color camo on a Meng 1/35 scale T-90A. A modern tank with full-length fender skirts, this model requires a different painting order.

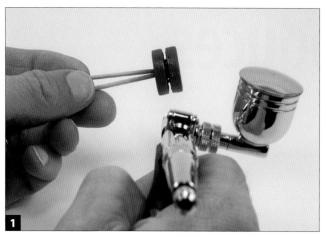

First, I painted the road-wheel tires. With the pressure at 15 psi, I sprayed the tires with Testors Model Master schwarzgrau. The low pressure allows the paint to get between the halves without flooding the surfaces.

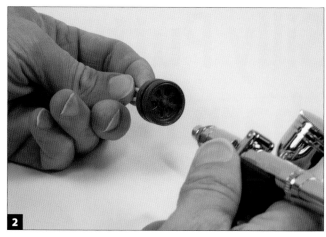

Next, I turned the wheels to face the brush and airbrushed the tire sidewalls with schwarzgrau.

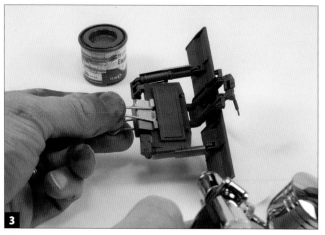

The T-90's dozer blade is a different color. I airbrushed it with Humbrol light green, taking special care to paint all the nooks and crannies, especially areas around the moving parts. Keeping the pressure at 15 psi minimized paint buildup as I passed over areas repeatedly.

Meng included a photoetched-metal mask for the road wheels. It's a simple matter to position the molded rim inside the opening and airbrush the wheels Humbrol dark green (No. 163) at 15 psi, which prevents paint from being forced past the stencil edge.

Keeping the mask tight against the wheel produces a beautifully painted road wheel. I repeated the process for each wheel, front and back.

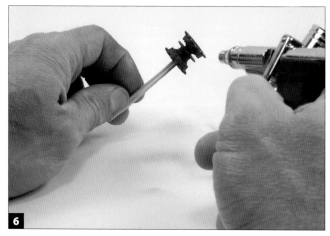

I painted the drive sprockets at the same time, turning them front and back to ensure proper coverage.

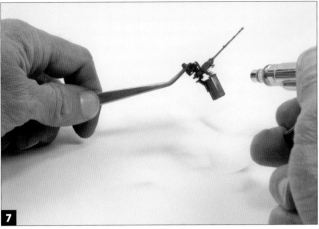

7 A pair of reverse tweezers made a gentle handle for the DShK 12.7mm machine gun. I painted the mount and ammunition box Humbrol dark green at 15 psi.

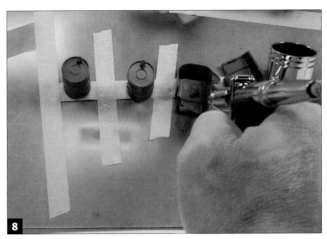

8 After taping the fuel tanks and front fender to cardboard, I painted them Humbrol dark green.

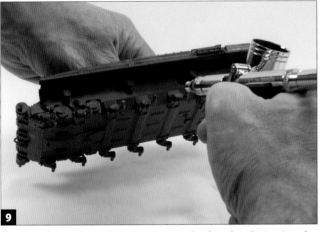

9 Because the tracks and fenders have to be fitted early, I painted the hull around the suspension Humbrol dark green.

10 I sprayed the enamel at 15 psi around the road wheel arms and the return roller. I then turned the pressure up to 25 psi to paint the larger sections of the hull and the underside of the fenders.

11 For painting the assembled individual link track runs, I darkened Tamiya metallic gray (XF-56) with NATO black (XF-69) and then added a few drops of NATO brown (XF-68). I set the pressure at 15 psi and sprayed just enough paint to cover the plastic without flooding the gaps between the links.

12 After installing the road wheels and the tracks, I added the fender skirts. To mask the tracks, I wrapped them with Tamiya tape. You don't need to press hard, just enough for the tape to stay in place.

13 To protect the wheels, I slid bits of paper under the skirts and tacked the paper in place with tape.

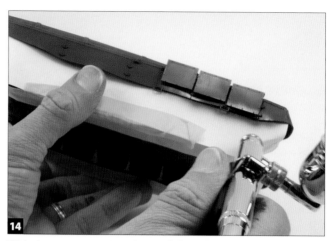

14 With the pressure at 12 psi, I carefully sprayed Humbrol dark green along the skirt edges to obtain even coverage with minimal risk of overspray. Then I dialed the pressure to 20 psi and sprayed the rest of the hull.

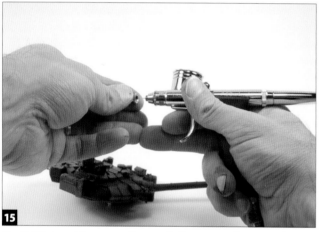

15 The T-90's turret is covered in standoff armor and stowage boxes. To make it easier to paint around and under those details, I removed the needle guard from the airbrush.

16 I began painting the turret by spraying under the explosive reactive armor blocks at 12 psi. It's important to get paint under them without flooding the surface.

17 There's a lot of intricate detail on the turret, so I took my time and carefully painted around it. With the needle guard off, you can get in close, just be careful not to hit the exposed needle on the plastic.

18 To mask with Silly Putty, first tear off a piece, flatten it, and stretch it out. The putty works best when it is thin enough to lay over detail but not so thin that it is transparent.

Place the Silly Putty on the model and push it around details. You can manipulate it with a finger or a tool such as a toothpick. You can use a single piece to mask an entire area.

You could also roll worms of the putty to outline an area, as I did on the turret. This technique works best when you have many fragile parts to go around that could be easily broken during masking or removal. You can cut Silly Putty with scissors to remove any excess.

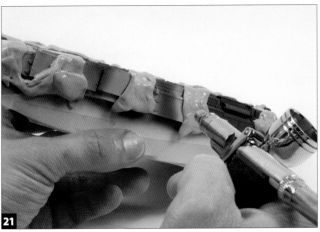

Once the Silly Putty was in place, I sprayed the next color, Humbrol cream (No. 103), along the masked edges at 20 psi.

I filled in the areas between the masks at 25 psi, but kept the pattern narrow to prevent paint from spraying past the masks. If you work slowly and pay attention, you can avoid mistakes.

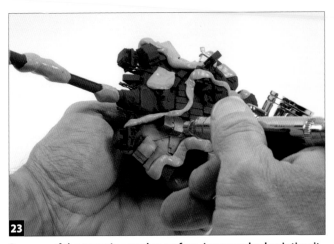

Because of the turret's complex surface, I approached painting it differently. I lightly sprayed cream from the inside out at 15 psi, gradually building up the density of the color.

To remove Silly Putty, simply grab hold of a piece and pull it off the surface. You can pick up recalcitrant putty by pressing a blob of it against the spot. It almost always sticks better to itself than to the model.

25

Here's another way to apply Silly Putty. Spread out a blob on a hard, smooth surface until it is about ¹⁄₁₆" thick. Then you can cut it with a new hobby knife blade.

26

Cut a strip approximately ½" wide and a little longer than the area to be masked. In this case, I'm masking an area of black on the front starboard fender.

27

I lifted the putty and pushed it gently against the surface to seal the mask.

28

After applying a second putty strip to outline the other side of the black strip, I refined the curves by pushing the Silly Putty into place with a metal probe.

29

I sprayed Humbrol flat black (No. 33) in the masked areas at 15 psi.

30

I swear, no matter how careful I am, there is always overspray that needs to be touched up. You can see a perfect outline of the Silly Putty masks on the tank's glacis plate.

31 I touched them up by spraying Humbrol cream at 12 psi in a fine pattern.

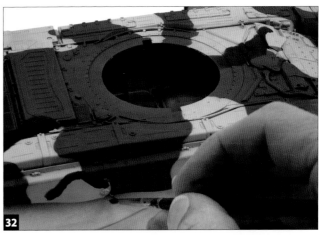

32 Some other touch-ups are better done by hand-brushing. I thinned the required colors with a little Humbrol thinner and painted the spots using the fewest strokes possible.

33 I sealed the enamels under thin layers of Testors Glosscote mixed with an equal measure of Testors Lacquer Thinner. This makes a good base for decals and weathering.

34 The kit's decals laid down over the gloss with a little help from Microscale Micro Set and Micro Sol decal solutions. The next day, I used a slightly damp cotton swab to remove the solutions' residue.

35 After spraying a wash of dark brown artist's oils thinned with Turpenoid and dry-brushing highlights, I airbrushed Testors Dullcote mixed with lacquer thinner.

36 Finally, using a tweezers, I removed the strips of tape that masked the tank's optics, dazzlers, and sights.

Poster putty leaves soft edges

S old under various brand names, including Blu Tack, Blue Stik, Sticky Fix Tak, Fun-Tak, and Handi-Tak, poster putty is a great masking material. Like Silly Putty, it stays in place on a model without damaging underlying paint. Unlike the hard-edged demarcation left by Silly Putty, poster putty produces a softer line. This makes it ideal for masking tightly sprayed camouflage patterns such as those found on U.S. military vehicles in NATO service and on many modern military aircraft. It's the perfect tool for painting the U.S. Air Force's 1960s camouflage, which was widely used during the Vietnam War. I built Academy's 1/48 scale F-4C Phantom II as flown by ace Col. Robin Olds, which featured this camouflage scheme. I finished it with decals from Furball Aero Designs.

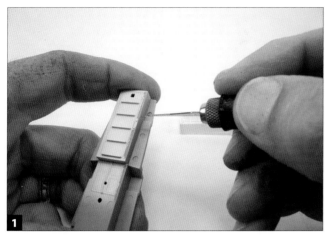

I airbrushed the parts for the landing gear wells and legs with Acrylicos Vallejo white primer before assembly because they were easy to reach. Paint interferes with glue, so I scraped the attachment surfaces with a knife.

I used Testors Metalizer exhaust on the engine fan parts that close the exhausts, but painted the front fans, which are visible through the model's long intakes, Metalizer dark anodonic gray (No. 1412).

When I started this project, I expected to use Model Master enamels for most of the painting. So I painted the inside of the intakes with insignia white (No. 1745), keeping the pressure at 15 psi to avoid producing strong vortices on the enclosed space. The light circles are putty-filled ejector-pin marks.

The kit features deep one-piece jet pipes with molded interior detail. I airbrushed them with Testors Metalizer exhaust (No. 1406) with the pressure at 12 psi, so I could keep spraying without flooding the surface.

I flowed an acrylic wash (a mix of Tamiya flat black, water, and a drop of dish soap to cut surface tension) into the engraved detail of the engine fans. This increases the contrast and makes the parts more visible through the small intakes.

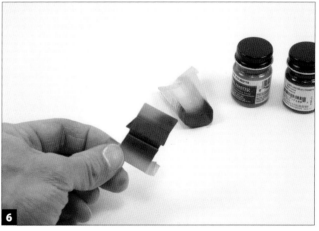

I masked the intakes with tape ½" inside the lips, and airbrushed on the exterior colors—dark green (No. 171004) for the port side, and dark tan (No. 1742) for the starboard intake.

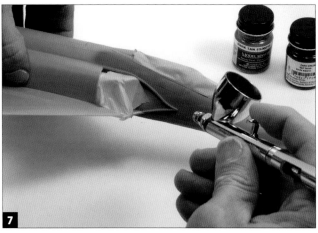

7 Don't forget to spray the fuselage behind the intakes. It's almost impossible to spray paint all the way into this spot once the intakes are attached.

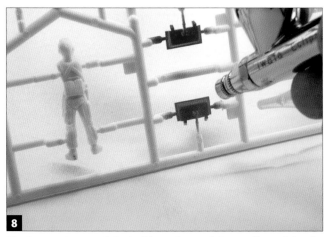

8 Moving on, I sprayed the inside surfaces of the auxiliary air intake doors insignia red, while they were still attached to the sprue.

9 After masking the canopy with a set from Furball Aero Designs, I attached the sections and sprayed the frame Model Master Acryl interior black (No. 4767). I then changed course and decided to paint the Phantom with acrylic paints from Hataka.

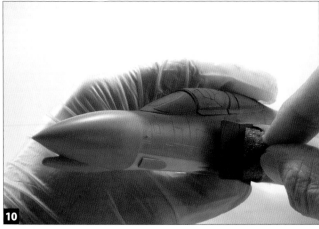

10 To protect the neatly painted intakes and exhausts, I masked them with foam rubber. I tore pieces slightly bigger than each opening and gently inserted them in the intakes so they filled the space and covered the previously painted color border.

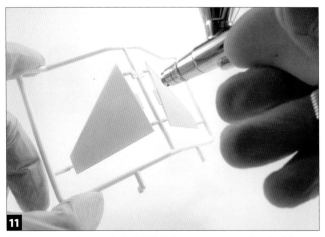

11 I base-coated the model with Vallejo gray primer mixed with several drops of Vallejo thinner and sprayed it at 25 psi. The horizontal stabilizers are best painted off the model to make finishing the natural-metal tail sections easier.

12 I had previously assembled the fuel tanks and primed them with the rest of the model.

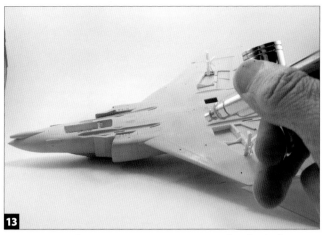

13 Hataka camouflage gray (No. HTK-A039) mixed with a little Vallejo thinner covered the underside of the airplane. Hataka's acrylic paints work best at 25–30 psi, so I kept the brush moving to prevent problems.

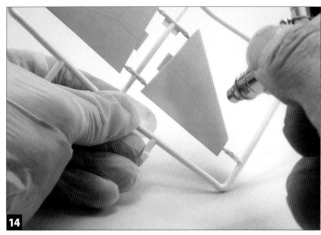

14 I made sure to paint all of the components while I had the paint in the brush. It's always a good idea to check the box and be sure you have all the parts that need the current color, including landing gear doors, air brakes, flaps, and pylons.

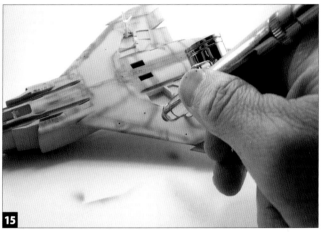

15 Vietnam War Phantoms can look pretty beat up. I added a few drops of Hataka night black (No. HTK-A041) to the light gray and sprayed the mix along panel lines under the airplane.

16 The shading was darker than I wanted, so I toned it down with a light overspray of straight camouflage gray.

17 To mask a model with poster putty, I first roll the putty into worms ¼–½" in diameter, with the outside surface as smooth as possible. The length should be just a little longer than the area to be masked.

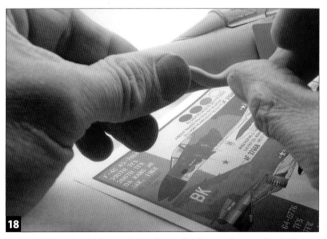

18 Press a putty worm into place along the line to be masked. The putty is very easy to push and bend to fit any shape, and not much pressure is required to stick it into place. The only caution is to avoid having the putty stick to itself, which it does better than sticking to the model.

19 I filled in behind the putty with tape, lightly pressing it to form a seal and prevent overspray from hitting unwanted spots.

20 As done with raised paper masks, spray perpendicular to the surface around the putty. Spraying toward the masks will produce harder lines.

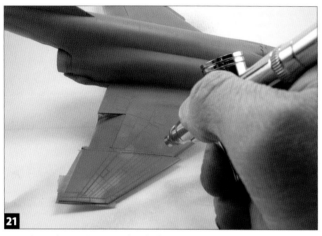

21 I continued painting Hataka dark tan (No. HTK-A012) over the upper surfaces of the Phantom at 30 psi. I added a few drops of camouflage gray and then post-shaded the panel centers.

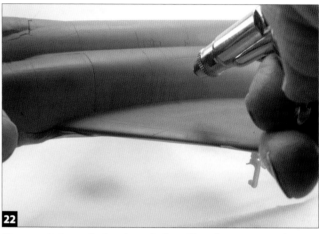

22 Many prototype photos show dark outlines for some panels on the fuselage at the wing root, so I mixed a couple of drops of night black into the dark tan and sprayed final lines.

23 The fast-drying Hataka acrylics end up with a gritty texture, especially around corners. The next day, I removed this with 1500-grit sandpaper, and eliminated the dust with a tack cloth.

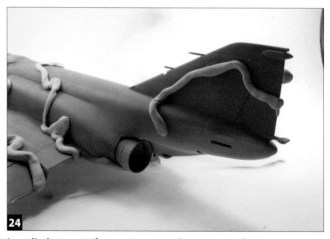

24 I applied worms of poster putty to the upper surfaces to mask the dark tan in preparation for airbrushing the next color, medium green.

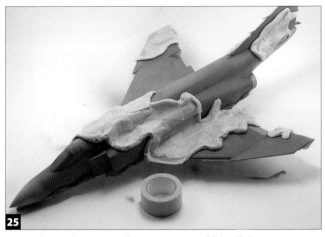

25 I pieced together strips of Tamiya tape to fill in all the areas behind the poster putty.

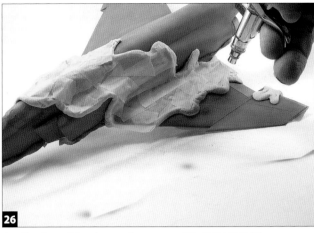

26 Application of Hataka medium green (No. HTK-A021) began along the poster putty. I sprayed a fine pattern to avoid excess paint building up along the masks.

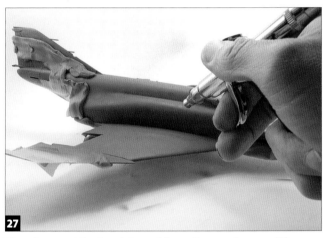

27 Then, I opened the brush to a wider pattern and sprayed the major color areas. Once it was dry, I lightly sanded the surface and rubbed it with a tack cloth.

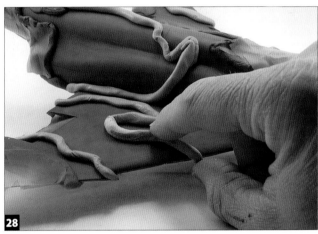

28 Another layer of color means more poster putty and tape. You'll notice that the color of the putty has changed. The Phantom is a good-sized airplane in 1/48 scale, and I ran out of the yellow putty that I started with.

29 The final color I sprayed was Hataka dark green (No. HTK-A016), starting along the masks and then filling in between.

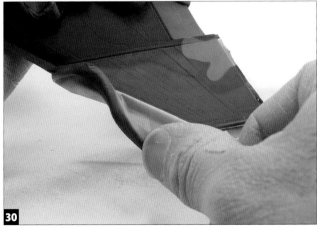

30 The moment of truth: I peeled off the tape and poster putty, revealing the three-color camouflage with soft edges.

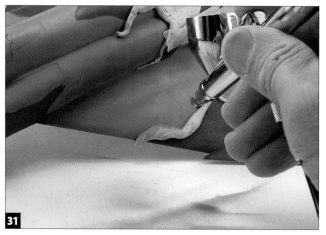

31 I touched up a couple of problem areas—from overspray and too-hard edges—by placing short poster-putty worms around them and airbrushing the colors.

32 To protect the acrylic paint from the Alclad II lacquers I planned to use for the metallic exhaust sections, I airbrushed the area with Pledge FloorCare Multi-Surface Finish. It works best in thin, quickly applied layers at 15 psi.

33 After masking, I base-coated the area with Alclad II airframe aluminum (No. AL119). This is a high-shine color that is usually applied over gloss black for full effect. Over other base coats, it produces a slightly weathered aluminum finish.

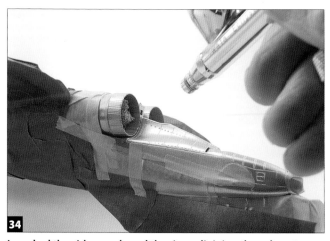

34 I masked the side panels and the ring adjoining the exhaust nozzles and airbrushed Alclad II dark aluminum (No. AL103). These metallic lacquers are airbrush-ready straight from the bottle and should be sprayed at 12–15 psi.

35 I covered the molded structural elements under the tail with thin strips of Tamiya tape.

36 I airbrushed Testors Metalizer titanium straight from the bottle at 15 psi on the center section of the horizontal stabilizers metal section.

37
The same dark titanium shade colored the exhaust section.

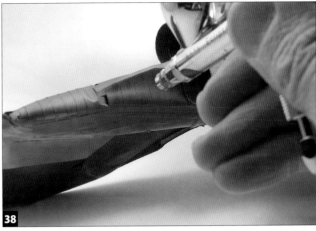

38
I added more contrast by airbrushing Testors Metalizer exhaust in the center of the panels directly behind the jet pipes as well as on the nozzles themselves.

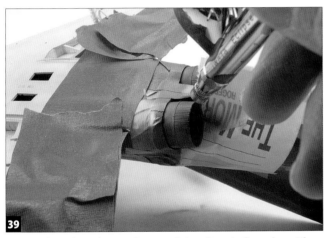

39
To complete the exhausts, I sprayed the aft end of nozzles with Testors Metalizer burnt iron. Tape covers the surrounding area, and scraps of paper slipped behind the nozzles protect against overspray.

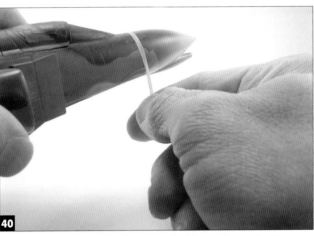

40
The nose of the F-4 is black, so I masked it starting with thin strips of tape to ensure alignment and conformity to the curves. More tape backed the area.

41
I airbrushed the radome with Hataka night black, starting along the tape edge.

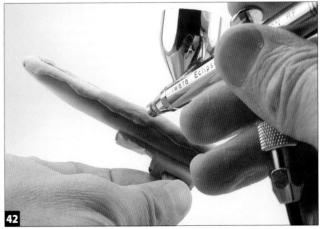

42
After masking the fuel tanks with poster putty, I airbrushed the upper halves with Hataka dark green.

43 I also painted the leading edges of the pylons. One is dark green, and the other is dark tan.

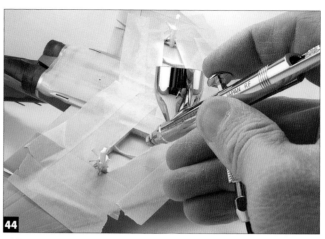

44 Although I had painted the wheel wells and main gear legs before construction, they had picked up a little overspray. I masked around them and airbrushed Tamiya flat white (XF-2) at 15 psi.

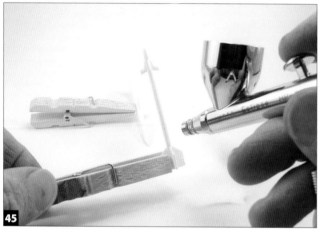

45 After assembling the Sidewinder and AIM-120 missiles, I painted them Tamiya flat white.

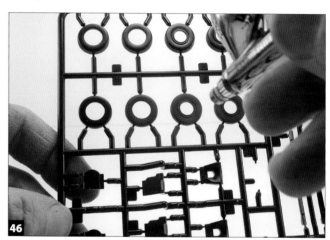

46 Academy molded the tires and wheels separately. Leaving them on the sprues, I painted the wheels Tamiya flat white and the tires Tamiya NATO black.

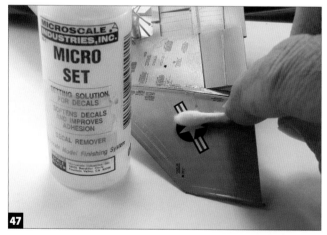

47 Between layers of Pledge, I applied the markings, which were a combination of decals from the kit and from Furball Aero Designs, with help from Microscale Micro Set. I followed them with a wash of dark brown artist's oils thinned with Turpenoid.

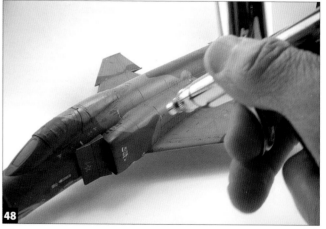

48 After spraying on a coat of Vallejo clear flat mixed with Vallejo thinner, I removed the masks from the canopies, added the details, and called the project done.

Freehanding camouflage on armor

PROJECT

12

German World War II armor is always a popular modeling subject, and part of the attraction is the variety of camouflage schemes applied to them. Beginning in 1943, German tanks, trucks, and self-propelled guns emerged from factories wearing an overall coat of dark yellow (or dunkelgelb). In the field, units were provided with red-brown and olive green pigment to be mixed with fuel or another solvent and applied to the vehicles with spray guns or brushes. The camouflage patterns used were the choice of the local commander or the crew. So for modelers, there are hundreds of designs from which to choose. I built Tamiya's 1/35 scale Marder IIIM and painted it a streaky camouflage pattern worn by a tank destroyer in France during 1944. The early stages of painting the open-top vehicle are different from painting a tank.

1

In order to paint the fighting compartment, I built the hull and the wall panel separately. I masked the attachment points with tape, so I wouldn't have to scrape them for assembly.

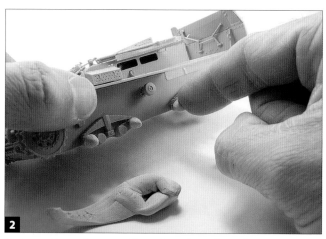

2

Poster putty conforms easily to the axle ends on the suspension, which makes it perfect for masking them.

3

I mixed 2 parts Tamiya dark yellow (XF-60) with 1 part Tamiya acrylic thinner, and painted the interior of the Marder at 15 psi. Spraying at this relatively low pressure made it easy to control the paint volume and the pattern, especially in the acute angle between plates.

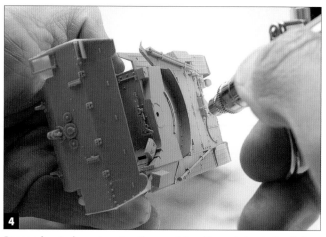

4

Remember to keep turning the model so the paint gets in all the areas that will be inaccessible when the compartment walls and gun are in place, such as the hull plating around the gun mount and inside of the splash plates in front of the gun.

5

I airbrushed the 7.5cm gun too, as it had a lot of hard-to-reach areas at the breech, mount, and controls. I took my time and painted very deliberately, checking and rechecking it from every angle to be sure it was completely painted.

6

I taped the armored walls and gun shield to cardboard for easier painting. They feature a lot of detail, so low pressure and a patient approach are required.

7

Before enclosing the fighting compartment, I hand-painted details, including the seats and radio, and weathered the interior with a dark brown artist's oil wash. This would have been difficult to do once the walls and gun were mounted.

8

After removing the tape masks, I carefully assembled the rest of the model by holding the parts in place and flowing Tamiya Extra Thin Cement into the seams with a fine brush. You need to work carefully because glue will ruin the paint. I left the wheels, exhaust, and some tools off for painting.

9

The next day, I was ready to paint the exterior. To protect the painted interior, I stuck Tamiya tape around the inside of the lip. More tape ensured that any overspray could not go anywhere.

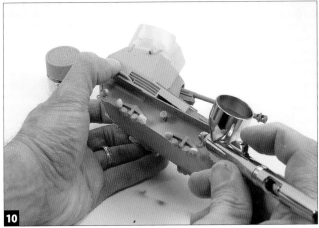

10

I mixed Tamiya dark yellow with thinner and airbrushed the exterior at 20 psi, starting with the running gear. Like any armor model, it pays to work slowly and carefully so all the details get painted.

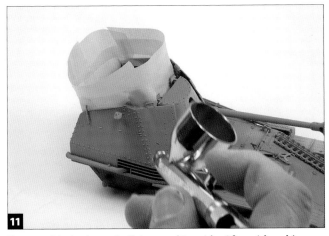

11

Happy with the lower hull, I moved topside. After airbrushing dark yellow along panel lines and into corners and crevices, I widened the pattern and covered the model. Be careful spraying around the tape to avoid pushing paint under the masks.

12

I had earlier assembled the idlers and sprockets, so I pressed them onto toothpicks and airbrushed them. However, I sprayed the road wheels on the sprue.

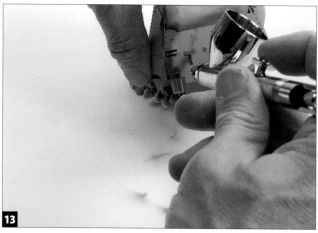

13 I let the paint dry for a day and then continued. I loaded the brush with a mix of equal parts Tamiya red brown (XF-64) and Tamiya thinner. To work close—within an inch of the surface—I removed the needle guard from the brush and set the pressure at 12 psi. I started each stripe in the middle.

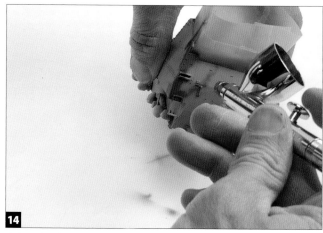

14 Using the thin paint and a lower pressure made it easier to control how much paint comes out. I kept the pattern narrow and laid down just a little paint at a time, gradually building the stripe.

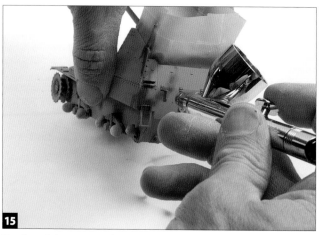

15 Don't rush it, or you risk making a mistake. Keep an eye on the photos or diagrams you use as reference to keep the pattern on track.

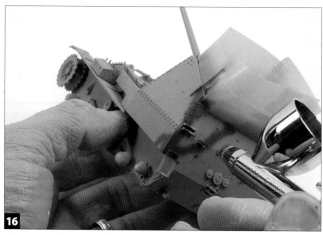

16 After several passes, the stripe was dense and well defined, so I could move on to the next stripe. This is time consuming, so be prepared to spend an hour or more painting a single color.

17 If you are unsure about following a diagram or want to be sure you get it right, draw the outline of the color on the paint with a pencil. This works best on a flat rather than gloss finish. I usually draw these areas slightly smaller than necessary to ensure that the marks get covered by paint.

18 Next, I added fine lines of Tamiya dark green (XF-61) mixed equally with Tamiya thinner. Spraying at 12 psi and working close kept the lines tight. At the same time, I painted the wheels with the camouflage colors.

Mistakes are inevitable. I airbrushed individual touch-ups with all three colors as necessary, cutting each with an equal measure of Tamiya thinner. I set the pressure at 12 psi.

Before adding decals and weathering, I sealed the acrylic paint with a generous layer of Pledge FloorCare Multi-Surface Finish built up in many thin layers airbrushed at 18 psi.

Every now and then, clear coats will blush during application as you can see here. It's often a warning that you might be laying the finish on a little thick. Set the model aside for a few hours and the blemish will more than likely disappear.

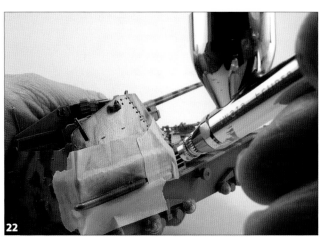

I let the Pledge set for 48 hours. Any less time than that and you risk leaving fingerprints or damaging it with tape. Then I masked the area around the exhaust with a mix of equal parts Tamiya hull red, NATO black, and gunmetal.

The muffler and the rest of the exhaust received the same color, a nice shade of old rust.

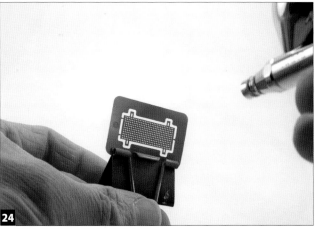

The kit includes a photoetched-metal muffler cover that I airbrushed dark yellow while it was still on the fret.

25

After attaching the exhaust to the Marder, I matched the cover to the surrounding camouflage with airbrushed stripes of red brown and dark green. I kept the pressure at 10 psi to avoid flooding the covers' tiny openings with paint.

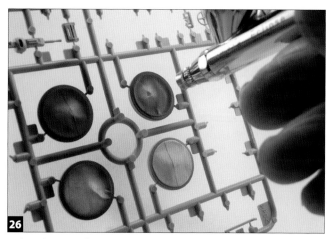

26

I placed strips of tape across the road wheels, and trimmed them to fit the rims by running the tip of a brand new No. 11 blade around the edge. Then I painted the tires with Tamiya NATO black at 15 psi.

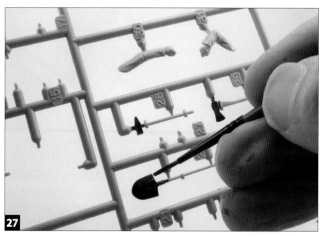

27

I hand-painted the tools that remained on the sprue. I mixed equal parts Tamiya NATO black and metallic gray (XF-56) for the metal parts. For the wooden handles, I used Vallejo old wood streaked with Vallejo new wood and then sealed them with Tamiya clear orange.

28

I painted other tools and the spare tracks on the model using Tamiya and Vallejo acrylics.

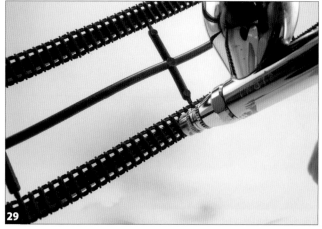

29

To create a look of heavy steel, I airbrushed the vinyl tracks with a mix of Tamiya metallic gray and hull red. I set the pressure at 20 psi to blow excess paint through the guide-horn holes and to prevent excess paint problems.

30

Dry-brushing the tracks with Tamiya flat aluminum produces the look of bare metal on the contact points.

31 After applying decals, I airbrushed the Marder with Tamiya clear flat at 20 psi to knock down the gloss of the Pledge.

32 I applied acrylic weathering colors from LifeColor, including two shades of European mud. I thinned the paints with LifeColor thinner and airbrushed them at 15 psi. The focus of these layers was around the suspension, wheels, and lower hull—anywhere dust and dirt kicked up by the tracks would be deposited.

33 For a layer of splattered mud, I mixed LifeColor Northern European mud with water and a drop of dish soap.

34 I picked the mud mix up with an old paintbrush, making sure that the bristles were pretty well saturated.

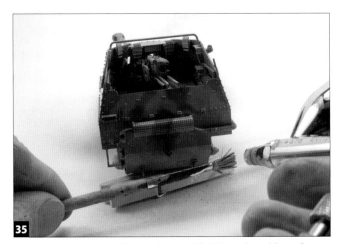

35 Holding the paintbrush near the model, I blew short blasts from the airbrush through the bristles to spatter droplets of mud over the surface. Less is more with this technique, so work slowly and when you think you need a little more, stop. It's easier to add more spatter than try to take it off.

36 I adjusted and fine-tuned the mud layer using a little water on a cotton swab. Stroking downward leaves an impression like rain. To complete the Marder, I installed the wheels and tracks.

Mottling a Luftwaffe fighter

One highlight of building World War II German fighters is selecting from a large variety of colors and camouflage. These schemes, especially the mid- and late-war mottled splotches, are among the most challenging to airbrush. During the war, the fine spots were applied at the factory or in the field with a spray gun, so it's appropriate to apply them with an airbrush. However, you are working in sizes much smaller than the original vehicles, and scaling the size of the spots and the density can be tough to master. It involves getting close to the model and having fine control, as I found out when painting Eduard's 1/48 scale Messerschmitt Bf 109E-7/Trop. The aircraft I modeled flew in North Africa and wore one of my favorite camouflage patterns—a desert sand color with dark green splotches.

1

I applied the kit's precut canopy masks to the clear parts before adding them to the fuselage. I glued the windshield and rear section in place, but tacked the middle section so I could display it open. After painting the RLM 02 interior color, it revealed a few gaps around the windshield that I filled and sanded.

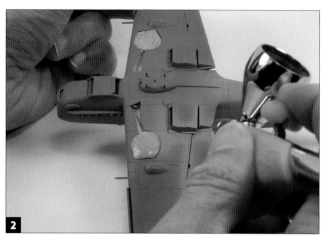

2

After masking the wheel wells with Silly Putty and tape, I airbrushed Model Master RLM 78 hellblau under the airplane, starting along the control surface edges and other recesses at 15 psi.

3

After the details were painted, I widened the pattern and turned the pressure up to 25 psi to finish the job. I lightened the color with a few drops of light gray to post-shade the panel centers.

4

Keep the instructions handy as a guide to help you get the paint everywhere it needs to go. On the Messerschmitt, I worked to ensure the hellblau extended as far up the fuselage sides as it needed to, overlapping the areas that would be sand color.

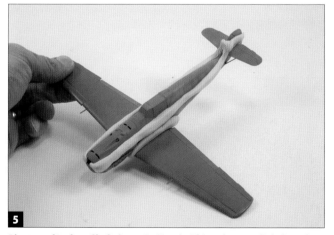

5

Photos of Luftwaffe fighters in North Africa show a slightly soft demarcation. I masked the blue with poster putty to produce this effect. Make sure to mask the roots of the wings and horizontal stabilizers to guard against overspray.

6

Keeping the pressure at 15 psi, I sprayed RLM 79 sandgelb over the wings. Using a lower pressure coats the model, but minimizes overspray on the fuselage sides and under the wings.

7 To spray sandgelb on the fuselage, hold the brush perpendicular to the surface and spray past the edge of the poster putty mask at 15 psi. Keep the brush moving steadily to avoid spraying too much paint in any one spot.

8 The spine of the fuselage proved challenging. I set the pressure to 12 psi, and keeping a narrow pattern, sprayed sandgelb just along the top of the surface. Move the brush forward and back along the fuselage, not side-to-side, and avoid spraying paint down into the gap at the edge of the mask.

9 Next, I post-shaded panel centers. I lightened the base sandgelb color quite a bit, reasoning that the actual paint would have faded considerably when exposed to desert sun and wind. The wings were easy to do, and I airbrushed several different shades at 15 psi.

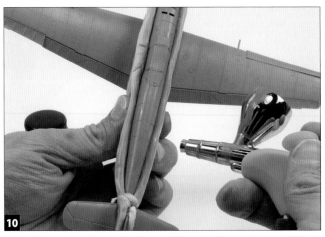

10 Completing the narrow fuselage with its masks was more difficult because I wanted to avoid spraying paint into the gap along the masked edges. I kept the pressure at 12 psi and moved the brush around the fuselage…

11 …so that the spray pattern was always perpendicular to the surface. This worked very well on the Bf 109's prominent rear fuselage panels.

12 Although I was being careful, after removing the masks, I noticed that some overspray reached the fuselage sides above the wing.

13 I loaded a brush with hellblau and airbrushed it to cover the blemishes. Then I set the model aside to dry for a couple of days.

14 Next came the fun part—spraying the dark green splotches. I thinned RLM 80 dark green slightly more than usual (about equal parts thinner and paint), dialed the pressure to about 12 psi, and removed the needle guard from the brush so I could get in close. Pulling back on the needle, I began by spraying a thin, tiny spot of paint.

15 I gradually built up the size and density of the spot. To do so, work slowly and don't be tempted to spray too much color at once. This is one of those times when it's easier to add more color rather than removing it.

16 If you have a large spot to add, try starting with one spot for a corner.

17 Then you can paint another small spot for the next corner.

18 Make one spot for each corner. Here, the splotch I'm painting is basically triangular.

19 With the extremities defined, it's easy to join them together. This ensures that the size and shape of the splotch matches the full-size object, or at least the model's painting diagrams.

20 Mistakes are inevitable. I fixed oversized green blobs, overspray, and splatters by airbrushing sandgelb at 12 psi. Be prepared to go back and forth a few times to refine the colors until you are happy with the results.

21 I masked the rear fuselage with Tamiya tape and then airbrushed Model Master flat white for the tail band. Keeping the pressure at 15 psi minimized the amount of paint pushed past the tape.

22 I let the paint cure for several days, so all the chemicals could gas out. Then I sealed the enamels with Pledge FloorCare Multi-Surface Finish sprayed at 20 psi and built up in layers.

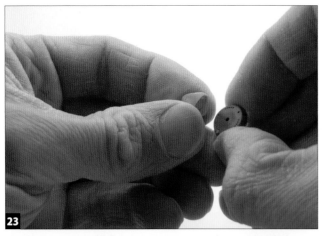

23 The kit's spinner, which comes in two parts that sandwich the prop, had to be painted red and white. I tacked the two sections together with poster putty to keep the alignment correct.

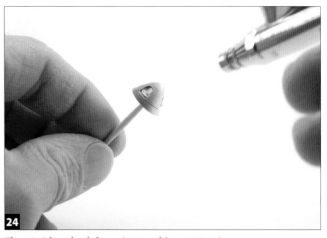

24 Then I airbrushed the spinner white at 20 psi.

25 Once the white was dry, I cut thin triangles of masking tape that ended in very narrow points. I used those to establish the outer edges of the white segment of the spinner and then filled the rest with more tape.

26 Next, I airbrushed the spinner RLM 04 rot at 20 psi. The white undercoat brightened the red.

27 Don't forget the landing gear. I painted the wheel hubs black, the separate tires dark gray, and the legs RLM 02 grau while on the sprues.

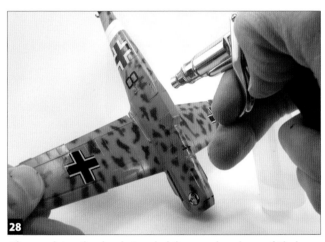

28 After applying the decals, I sealed them under a layer of Pledge sprayed just over the markings. This protects them from the artist's oil washes and other weathering that followed.

29 Once I had all the weathering done, I sprayed several thin layers of Testors Acryl clear flat over the model to dull the shine and unify all the finishes. Although airbrush-ready straight from the bottle, I find Acryl paints benefit from adding a few drops of Testors Universal Acrylic Thinner.

30 Some exhaust staining was the last step before unmasking the canopy and final assembly. I added several drops of Testors Acrylic black to the clear flat, thinned at about 40 percent with Testor acrylic thinner. I sprayed the mixture in thin layers arcing back from the exhausts across the wing root.

Airbrushing big-scale figures

PROJECT
14

Kits of creatures and characters from movies and television, especially science fiction and horror, have been a part of scale modeling since the first plastic kits hit the market in the 1950s. From the days of Aurora's Universal Studios monsters to the vinyl kits of Batman in the late 1980s to today's high-tech kits from Moebius, Polar Lights, and Dragon, they have remained popular. I've always loved the subject matter, but blending oils or acrylics on the surface with a paintbrush never came easily. Then I discovered that an airbrush can do most of the work and that I could adapt my techniques for painting armor and aircraft to figures. That's exactly what I did with Moebius's 1/6 scale Bride of Frankenstein. This kit recreates a scene from the climax of the famous movie.

After spraying all the parts with Vallejo gray primer, I airbrushed the monster's head with a base coat mixed from Tamiya deck tan, buff, and a few drops of olive green. The olive green gives the reanimated creature a deathly and unearthly tone. I mixed more than I needed for the base coat and poured it in two containers.

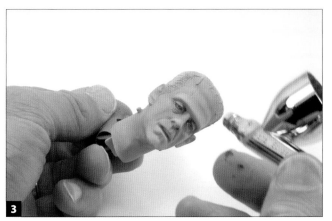

I darkened the paint in one container with a few more drops of olive green. Angling the head away from me, at 12 psi, I sprayed the underside of details such as the chin, nose, lips, brow, ears, and forehead furrows. The key is imagining how light would fall on the details; the darker areas are under overhangs.

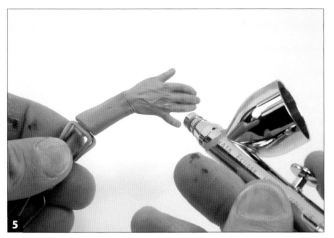

I added a few more drops of olive green and a little more thinner, and then sprayed the finer lines in the shadows. As you can see in the photos, I used binder clips to hold the parts as I airbrushed them.

The other areas of flesh, including the monster's hands, received the same base color as the head. The darker colors help define details like hands, especially where the fingers are molded together.

To further "corpsify" the creature, I mixed several drops of red into some thin base color and airbrushed this color around the knuckles…

…as well as the scars and blemishes on his face. Spraying at a low pressure, it is easy to control the volume of paint hitting the surface, so you can add fine lines and faint discoloration. One of the best things about painting fantasy figures is that there are few rules, so you can have fun and experiment.

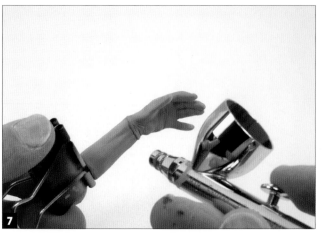

7

You can produce shadows on skin by adding a little blue to the flesh color. It doesn't take much, so start by putting a few drops in a small paint cup filled with the flesh paint. You can always add more if it's too light. I sprayed this mix under the creature's arm and hand. Think about the areas where direct light doesn't reach.

8

While working on the hands, I flipped them over and sprayed the bluish tint over the molded-in veins. This adds a nice unearthly feel to the creature.

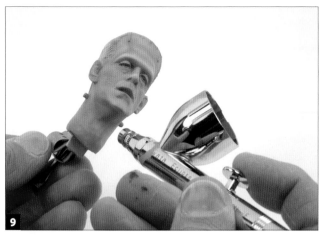

9

The blue also darkened the areas under the creature's chin, throat, and ears. I sprayed a thin layer around the neck where it goes into the collar because it will be in shadow on the finished model.

10

I sprayed the blue tint under the jutting brow, building up the color in the corners of the eye sockets.

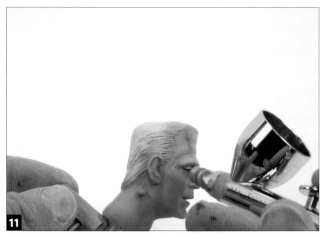

11

A little blue also deepens the creases in his face and those around his mouth and the outside of his eyes.

12

I mixed a few drops of Tamiya blue into flat black to color the creature's hair. I could have masked the hairline, but I thought it would be better freehand. The key is to always spray away from the edge, so the tightest part of the pattern falls along it.

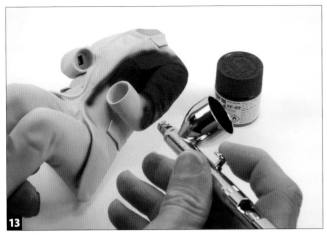

13 Black and white are two of the hardest colors to shade because they are natural extremes. For the creature's black suit, I started with a base coat of Tamiya NATO black (XF-69), which is actually a dark gray. For best coverage, I airbrushed the suit at 20 psi and started with the creases.

14 I then mixed a few drop of light gray into NATO gray and sprayed it along the upper surfaces, starting with the shoulders. You want to create highlights where light would fall on the suit. I dialed the pressure back to 12 psi and added a little more thinner, so I could better control the density of the paint.

15 I continued with the lighter shade, spraying fine, thin lines on the upper sides of folds and creases on the jacket and pants. Patience is a virtue here—speed can cause overspray or missed areas.

16 I emptied the paint reservoir but didn't clean it out. I poured in a little Tamiya flat back (XF-1) and thinner, and sprayed recesses including the line between the creature's legs to create shadows.

17 Angling the airbrush up, I sprayed black under the folds in the clothing. Combined with the highlights sprayed earlier, the creature's suit became more realistic as the different tones mixed.

18 For some variety, I airbrushed the shirt Tamiya German gray at 12 psi, leaving NATO black around the edges to show shadows of the jacket lapels.

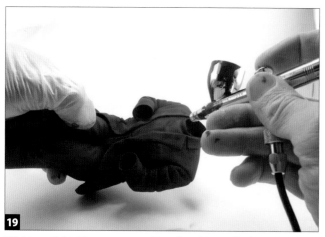

19 I lightened the German gray with a few drops of light gray and airbrushed the upper edges of folds and creases in the shirt.

20 The monster's boots should be dark brown—and a little dirty. I mixed Tamiya flat earth and NATO black and airbrushed the oversized footwear at 20 psi. Then I mixed in about 30 percent more flat earth and sprayed highlights on the toes.

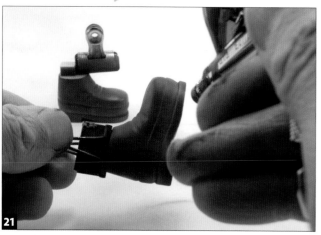

21 Since the creature wanders the countryside through much of the movie, his boots are going to be dirty. I mixed Tamiya buff with clear flat and thinner, and sprayed this dusty shade along the sides of the boots, focusing along the edge of the sole.

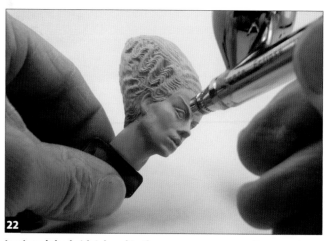

22 I painted the bride's head in the same sequence as the monster but using a different base coat. Elsa Lanchester's makeup was more human looking, so I started with a mix of equal parts Tamiya flesh and buff. Here, I'm painting her cheeks with the base color mixed with a few drops of red.

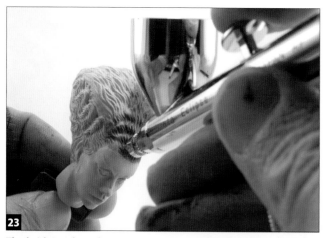

23 The bride's auburn hair started with an airbrushed base coat of Tamiya hull red lightened with a few drops of buff. By keeping the pressure low, at 12 psi, I was able to easily spray a sharp line along the hairline.

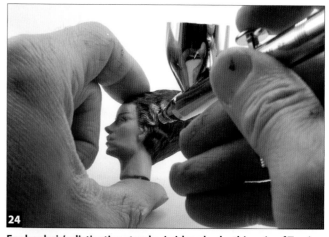

24 For her hair's distinctive streaks, I airbrushed a thin mix of Tamiya flat white and a few drops of light gray at 12 psi in a very fine pattern. I also used the same color to airbrush her eyes.

25 I applied a wash of burnt umber artist's oils thinned with Turpenoid to enhance the shadows between strands. Then I gave the creature's hair a wash of black artist's oils.

26 A wash of blood red artist's oils thinned with Turpenoid brought the scars on the bride's chin to sickening life, while I used a purple wash on the creature's scars.

27 There are some details you can't paint with an airbrush. I hand-painted the bride's eyebrows and liner with a dark red-brown (a mix of hull red and black). Her lips are a mix of Tamiya red and hull red, and her teeth are white. I used a mix of olive green and yellow for her irises. On the creature, I painted his eyes Tamiya flat brown, and he has no eyebrows.

28 I dry-brushed the creature's hair medium gray, and then the bride's hair with Tamiya flat red. The streaks in her bouffant were dry-brushed with flat white. You can also see the catch lights in her eyes. These small dots of white, applied in the same spot in each eye, mimic light reflecting off the eyeballs and add life to a figure.

29 I airbrushed both heads with Tamiya flat white to give the hair and flesh a realistic sheen.

30 Finally, I hand-brushed Tamiya clear gloss over the eyes and lips. A wash of thin red acrylics gave the eyes a nice rheumy appearance.

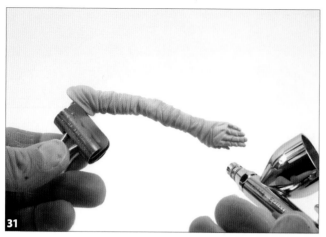

31
The bride's arms came next. I painted them with a mix of equal parts Tamiya buff and deck tan.

32
I added a few drops of flat earth to the base color mix and airbrushed it in fine thin lines along the edges of the bandages on the arms. A dark brown artist's oil wash and dry-brushing with white finished the arms.

33
Tradition dictates that brides wear white, and the monster's mate is no exception. I wanted white to be the highlight color for her dress, so I sprayed a base coat of 90 percent white and 10 percent deck tan.

34
I deepened shadows in and under the dress folds by airbrushing a mix of 80 percent white and 20 percent buff. A slightly darker shade followed in the deepest spots. After cleaning the brush, I sprayed pure white along the peaks of the folds and shoulders.

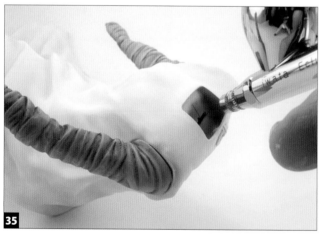

35
The neck of the dress is deep, so I airbrushed Tamiya German gray into it for shadows. Working close at 10 psi prevented overspray.

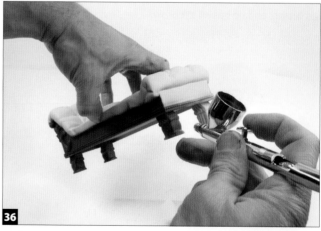

36
With the happy couple completed, I moved to the décor. The lounge has a carved wooden base, which I base-coated with a mix of 60 percent Tamiya hull red and 40 percent dark brown. There is much detail to spray around, so I kept the pressure at 15 psi.

37 I darkened the wood mix with a little black and sprayed around the edge of the relief carvings as well as along the border of the upholstery. This creates shadows as well as the appearance of collected varnish around the details.

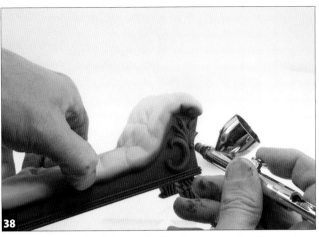

38 I sprayed base color, lightened with a few drops of yellow, onto the tops of the carvings to produce highlights. I used a fine pattern at 12 psi. Angling the brush low so the spray was almost perpendicular to the surface, I sprayed the highlight color over the trim along the lower edge of the frame.

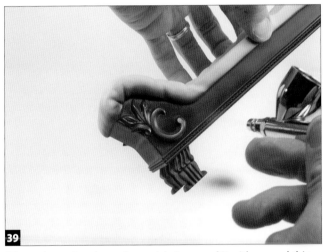

39 All good woodwork needs varnish. I sprayed it with several thin layers of Tamiya clear yellow gloss, gradually building up a deep, warm shine.

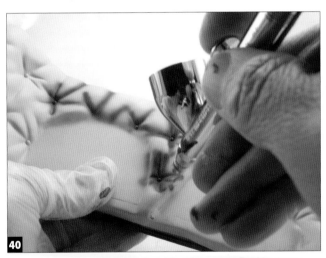

40 I pre-shaded the upholstery by airbrushing thin flat black into the creases around the buttons at 15 psi. This doesn't need to be perfect, and it should be darkest and densest at the center.

41 After masking off the finished woodwork, I airbrushed a mix of 60 percent hull red and 40 percent flat red over the upholstery. I started in the centers of the areas between the creases, filling them in as I worked out to the pre-shading.

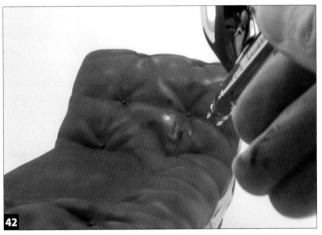

42 Building up the density of the color, I kept it thin over the creases, allowing a hint of black to show, which provided the upholstery with some variety.

43

I improved the upholstery's appearance by mixing a few drops of yellow into the mix and airbrushing the tops of the molded bulges. This post-shading helped the material look more like plush leather.

44

I pre-shaded the wall acting as the backdrop by airbrushing flat black along the mortar between the bricks. More flat black sprayed along the edge of the stones gave the diorama a nice finished look.

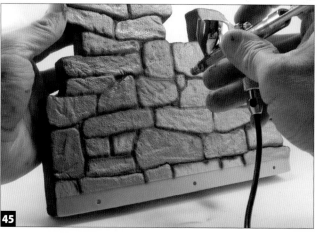

45

Then I sprayed the wall's individual blocks several shades of gray and tan mixed with Tamiya acrylics. Most of them are similar—mixed using medium sea gray as a base—but throwing in some with different colors makes the wall visually interesting. I sprayed the stones freehand at 15 psi, misting the color over the pre-shading.

46

A wash of black artist's oil paint and Turpenoid enhanced the texture of the rocks and softened the contrast between the colors.

47

To differentiate the platform from the lounge's wooden base, I airbrushed it with hull red straight from the bottle.

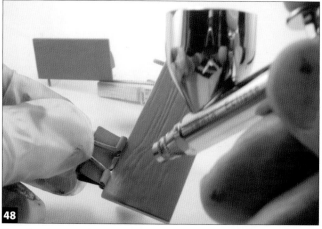

48

To paint the wooden shelves that go on the wall, I mixed a little red brown into flat earth. A subsequent wash of brown artist's oils emphasized the molded grain.

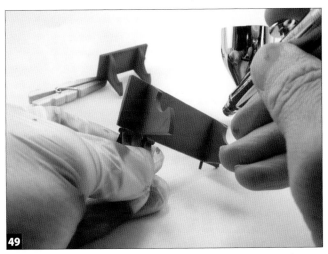

49 I darkened the wood color with a little more red-brown and airbrushed shadows around the shelves' brackets.

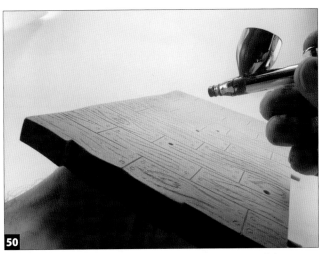

50 After spraying the edge of the floor flat black, I painted the wooden planks with Tamiya buff. Spraying from the center of the floor back across the edges at a low angle prevents overspray that could mar the black border.

51 Spraying at 12 psi, I outlined each plank with fine lines of the flat earth and red-brown mix I used for the shelves.

52 A heavy wash of ochre artist's oils thinned with Turpenoid settled into the molded grain of the floor and slightly darkened its light wood color.

53 Then I flowed a burnt umber wash along the gaps between the planks to add more depth.

54 Finally, I dry-brushed the floor with Tamiya deck tan and then hand-painted the nails German gray.

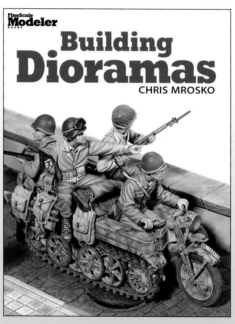
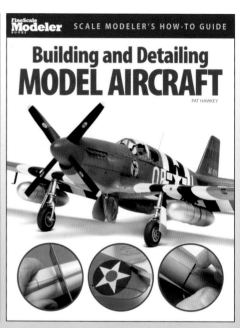